W9-CPF-611

COUNTRY LIVING'S

GUIDE TO
THE BEST
FLEA MARKETS

COUNTRY LIVING'S

GUIDE TO
THE BEST
FLEA MARKETS

How to Find (and Bargain for) Antiques and
Other Treasures in the U.S. and Canada

Text by Marie Proeller

HEARST BOOKS

New York

Copyright © 2002 by Hearst Communications, Inc.

All rights reserved. No part of this book may be reproduced or utilized in any form or by any means, electronic or mechanical, including photocopying, recording, or by any information storage and retrieval system, without permission in writing from the Publisher. Inquiries should be addressed to Managing Editor, Hearst Books, 959 Eighth Avenue, New York, N.Y. 10019.

Library of Congress Cataloging-in-Publication Data

Proeller, Marie.
    Country living guide to the best flea markets : how to find (and bargain for) antiques and other treasures in the U.S. and Canada / by Marie Proeller.
        p.cm.
    Includes index.
    ISBN 1-58816-017-3
    1. Antiques—United States—Directories. 2. Antiques—Canada—Directories. 3. Flea markets—United States—Directories. 4. Flea markets—Canada—Directories. I. Country living (New York, N.Y.) II. Title.

NK1127.P76 2002
381'.457451'02573—dc21   2001039861

First Edition

1 2 3 4 5 6 7 8 9 10

Printed in China

For *Country Living*
Editor-in-Chief Nancy Mernit Soriano
Art Director Susan M. Netzel
Deputy Editor Lawrence A. Bilotti

Cover photograph by Alan Richardson
Back cover photograph by Keith Scott Morton

Edited by Sarah Zwiebach
Designed by Alexandra Maldonado

www.countryliving.com

Contents

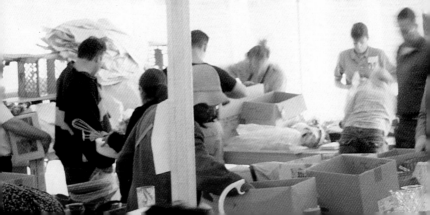

Foreword

If someone were to ask me to name my favorite pastime, flea marketing would certainly be at the top of the list. As a collector, homemaker, and editor of one of the leading decorating/lifestyle magazines in America, I have delighted in shopping flea markets from coast to coast and, on several occasions, London and Paris. Along the way I have added to existing collections, started a few new ones, and filled my home—and the homes of friends and family—with unique objects, gifts, and furnishings. For me, each flea market "find" carries its own special memory of place, time, and experience.

In this book, we share many of these experiences with you by providing a comprehensive guide to the best flea markets in North America. Within each chapter you'll discover key markets in every region of the country (Canada as well) with special "insider tips" on where the sales are and what you're likely to find at each location. We've included a state-by-state, province-by-province listing of more than 200 flea markets, with specific addresses, times of operation, telephone numbers, Web sites (when available) and specialties, if any. And for those of you planning a day trip or weekend, there is additional information on other local shopping opportunities, restaurants, and great places for an overnight stay.

Nancy Mernit Soriano
Editor-in-Chief
Country Living

How to Use This Guide

Country Living's Guide to The Best Flea Markets is a whole
new kind of resource for anyone under the spell of these
bountiful bazaars. Designed to appeal to the casual collector
as well as the seasoned flea market attendee, this volume goes
far beyond just telling you where the best sales are: It also
reveals how to spot treasures, negotiate the best prices, even
plan a weekend around a big sale. Most exciting, an easy-to-
tote size and a place to take notes will help you keep and use
the information you need.

   We begin with Flea Markets 101, a crash course in flea
marketing. Not sure what to bring with you? Consult our
checklist before you go. Always been shy about asking for a
better price? We'll explain how to do it with tact. Is that $20
Roseville vase the real thing? Our tips will help you avoid
fakes and forgeries.

   Next we tell you where the sales are. We've divided the
book into six regions—New England, Middle Atlantic, South,
Midwest, West, and Canada. In each section you'll find three
highlighted sales followed by a listing of antiques and flea
markets in additional states. For each highlighted sale we not
only provide you with the dates, hours, and contact information,
but also delve deeper to uncover the history of the sale, the kinds

of collectibles you're likely to find there, and where the regulars love to shop, eat, and stay nearby.

Perhaps what makes this book most special is that more than two decades of experience are condensed within its covers. Each and every page is infused with the recommendations and hard-earned knowledge of the numerous dealers, collectors, decorators, and designers who we've been privileged to work with since *Country Living* first hit newsstands in 1978. (Our 100 favorite antiques and flea markets are listed on page 176. How many have *you* been to?)

Antiques sales and flea markets come in all shapes and sizes these days, from 25 dealers in an open field to 1,500 in a climate-controlled convention center. But they all have one thing in common: a prize waiting just for you. Happy treasure hunting!

— Marie Proeller

Flea Markets 101

Shopping at flea markets can be an enjoyable afternoon ramble as well as an economical way to decorate your home. However, the experience can also be overwhelming if you don't plan ahead. Here are some tips to help you shop like a pro.

What to Bring When You Go

> Clothing that you can layer and don't mind getting dirty.

> Comfortable shoes.

> Sunscreen, sunglasses, and a brimmed hat if you are attending an outdoor market.

> A roomy tote bag packed with items like hand wipes, bottled water, cell phone, pen, paper, and bubble wrap if you collect delicate pieces such as pottery.

> A flashlight if you're planning to arrive before sunrise.

> A tape measure and dimensions if you're looking for something to fit a particular space.

> A magnifying glass to examine hallmarks and small pieces, particularly pottery, glass, and jewelry.

> Up-to-date price guides to help you recognize a bargain and avoid overpaying.

> Bungee cords to secure the trunk lid or items on the roof rack if you're driving home, and old blankets to wrap up your purchases.

When to Arrive

The best time to attend a flea market depends on what your intentions are for the day. If one-of-a-kind pieces are what you're after, you must arrive at the crack of dawn; one dealer calls it "flashlight early." At most sales around the country, serious collectors arrive and begin negotiating prices before the dealers have even finished unpacking their trucks. The admission for arriving early can be more than the general admission and is noted here as "early-bird."

On the other hand, the best bargains are generally found at the end of the day, so feel free to sleep late if they are your quest. Dealers aren't fond of repacking their wares—especially large objects—and carting them home, so they will often let pieces go for less than they were originally asking. If a sale day has been particularly slow—owing to inclement weather, for instance, or a seasonal antiques show in the area that has kept regular customers away from a weekly venue—dealers will be even more eager to make a sale.

If casual perusing is all you're in the mood for, any time of the day will do. Midday is known to be a flea market's quietest time, when it is frequented only by people out for an afternoon stroll. Most collectors and antiques dealers have already come and gone, and others will be back at the end of the day, so the crowds are smaller.

Spotting a Prize

One of the main draws of flea market shopping is the possibility of finding a "sleeper," a treasure that everyone else has somehow skipped over. Although it's not a given that you'll spot a sleeper at each sale you attend, there are certain steps you can take to improve your chances of unearthing one. The first thing to do is to scour every inch of the dealer's space. Don't concentrate just on the items placed in full view on top of a table; rummage through boxes under the table, plow through piles of linens, and scan stacks of books. These are the places where wonderful pieces are often hidden.

Another thing to keep an eye out for as you walk through a market is the piece that looks out of place in a particular booth. For example, if an architectural salvage dealer happened upon a rare Depression glass pitcher, he would likely set it out between the corbels and pilasters and price it

far lower than it is actually worth. The same pitcher in the booth of a dealer knowledgeable in glassware will likely be marked at its full market value.

Once you've spotted something you love, act fast. Don't take a chance and walk through once more to think about it, because it's likely that the piece won't be there when you return. People strolling through a sale tend to glance at the pieces other people are holding in their hands, so chances are good your discovery will soon be spotted by others.

Final words of advice: Perfect your poker face. Say you've just spotted an incredibly rare Victorian sterling-silver napkin ring in the $1 box of silver-plated tableware. Resist the urge to gasp and clutch your friend's arm for support. Rather, calmly walk to the dealer, show her where you found the piece, pay, and be on your way. Be sure to wait until you're out of the dealer's earshot before celebrating.

Avoiding Fakes

Cleverly aged reproductions often make their way into flea markets. Sometimes these pieces are clearly marked as new, but just as often they are unmarked and placed side by side with the real thing, making it difficult for the casual collector to tell the difference. If unsure about the age of an object you're interested in buying, examine the piece closely and look for wear consistent with use. For instance, an antique dresser should exhibit concentrated wear around the drawer pulls, and the stretchers on a 19th-century wooden chair should be noticeably scuffed where feet have rested over the years. An evenly distressed surface without random nicks or dents should raise eyebrows and probably be avoided.

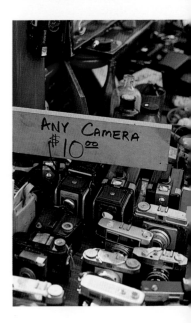

Second, learn as much as you can about the items you like to collect. Read books and magazine articles and view authentic pieces in museums and at antiques shows whenever possible. Once you become familiar

with the real thing—the manner in which glaze is applied to a McCoy vase or the effect of the elements on a Victorian cast-iron garden urn, for instance—reproductions become easier to spot.

Finally, ask as many questions as you can. Dealers, especially those who specialize, can teach you a lot about a subject and will often enthusiastically point out the details that make a piece authentic. Be wary of dealers who cannot tell you much about an object's age or provenance. If they merely tell you, "It's old," or can't recall the specifics about where they found the piece, keep walking. The old saying "If it looks too good to be true, it probably is" is worth bearing in mind.

Decorating a Particular Room

If you are searching for items to fit a special space in your home, consider the following: Many people remember to bring the dimensions of the space where they would like to put a sofa or daybed, but most forget the dimensions that are just as important—those of the doorway of the room and the entryway of the house. Collectors often swap stories about the wonderful bureau or bed frame that wouldn't fit through their door. It is also a good idea to bring snapshots of the room where the new object will go as well as paint samples and fabric swatches of upholstered pieces that will share the same setting.

How to Haggle

Many people are shy when it comes to asking for a lower price. But if you were to tag along with an antiques dealer on a buying run, you'd be amazed at the ease with which he bargains with colleagues. It's part of the game for dealers and they have come to expect it. In fact, prices at antiques and flea markets generally have approximately a 10-percent margin factored in so that dealers can be flexible with interested buyers.

The easiest and most polite way to negotiate a figure is to ask, "Is this your best price?" At the worst, the dealer can stand firm. On the whole, however, dealers will lower their prices to some degree. Another way to go about it is to propose a lower price than the one that is marked. In this scenario, however, it is important to suggest a fair price. For example, if an object is marked $20, you might offer the dealer $15, and she might meet you halfway and let you have it for $17. An offer of $10 for a $20 object will likely insult the dealer and make her unwilling to negotiate further. If you

are interested in more than one item at a particular booth, you could also ask if the dealer can do any better if you were to buy the entire group. This is a common method for antiques dealers, who frequently buy in bulk.

The one time to consider buying an item outright without haggling is if you spot something that you know to be an incredibly good deal. Perhaps the dealer knows what he has and is simply trying to get it off his hands; bargaining in this case may cause the dealer to rethink his generous offer. On the other hand, the dealer may be unaware of the true value of the piece, in which case you've found yourself a sleeper.

Payment Options

At most flea markets around the country, cash is the payment of choice. Bring small bills with you, if possible, as it can often be difficult for dealers to make change, particularly toward the

end of the day. Dealers will occasionally take local checks, especially when they offer pieces—such as large furniture or architectural salvage—with price tags of $300 or more. To date, credit cards have not been widely used at flea markets, although a few dealers do accept them. You should expect to pay a premium of 5 percent or more when using credit cards.

Packing and Delivery

By and large, flea market dealers do not deliver the wares that they sell. When they do offer this service, an additional fee will generally be charged (usually about $20 to $50 depending on the distance and how many flights of stairs lead to your home). If you are shopping for large pieces of furniture and do not own a car with a roomy interior or a roof rack, you may want to borrow a friend's car or rent a small moving van. For small pieces, dealers usually provide newspaper and plastic shopping bags. If you collect delicate items such as porcelain or glassware, you may want to bring bubble wrap and sturdier bags with you just to be safe.

Flea Market Ethics

Attend enough sales and you're sure to witness, or participate in, at least one heated argument over an object. Who saw it first? How long is a dealer obliged to hold an item while a buyer runs to find a cash machine? Though there's no way to ensure that these scuffles won't occur, the following guidelines will come in handy if you ever find yourself in such a situation.

Whoever sees an item first is generally the person to whom it should go. In the event that two parties really do see an object at exactly the same time, the proceedings can sometimes become an auction of sorts: At the dealer's discretion, the object often goes home with the highest bidder.

If you are interested in an object, pick it up and carry it with you while you browse the other items on the table. If you leave it on the table to look at something else, you forfeit your rights to the object. If you turn around to find someone else examining your treasure, you are at that person's mercy: She might take pity and give you the object back, but if she has fallen in love with it and is willing to commit on the spot, you are out of luck. And in the event that there is a group of objects being sold as a set, ownership goes to the person willing to buy the entire set rather than the person lobbying for just part of it.

If you cross paths with a flea market adversary who is either unaware of or unwilling to follow these unspoken rules of the game and you lose the battle as a result, don't lose heart; even the most seasoned collectors have similar stories to tell. Chalk it up to experience and know that you will likely laugh about it in the future.

New England

Where the Sales Are

Brimfield Antique Shows

BRIMFIELD, MASSACHUSETTS

Where > Various locations in and around Brimfield

When > Three times a year, in May, July, and September;
Tuesday through Sunday, individual hours vary

Admission > None

For more information > (413) 283-2418; www.brimfieldshow.com

Brimfield is no ordinary outdoor antiques market: It's a phenomenon. Held three times a year, in May, July, and September, this six-day extravaganza attracts some 30,000 treasure hunters to a sleepy New England village nestled in the foothills of the Berkshires. Nearly a dozen separate shows—featuring the best in country furniture, trade signs, pottery, textiles, and toys—stagger their openings, maintaining a steady sense of anticipation throughout the week. At each new opening, eager collectors mass outside the gates, often surrounded by local, national, and international news teams who are covering the event. When the gates finally open, it's a mad dash toward the booths, with many collectors literally running through the show from one table to the next searching for a prize.

If you plan to attend only one event, insiders report that there are slight differences between the three: May—the year's first—often features the premium pieces as well as premium prices; July's heat usually keeps the peak crowds at home, which means fewer dealers, but also fewer competitors; and September can sometimes yield great year-end bargains.

For those who have never been, the show's Web site, www.brimfieldshow.com, and the $5 visitor's guide published by the Quaboag Valley Chamber of Commerce (413-283-2418) both offer helpful tips. Seasoned attendees are also forthcoming with advice; one regular prepares what meals she can to avoid the crowds that take over the town's restaurants and cafés.

Brimfield alumni, you may notice, almost always describe their physical exhaustion and aching feet in detail, then break into smiles and tell you they wouldn't miss it for the world.

During the shows, lodging in the Brimfield area is booked for at least a 20-mile radius. Many people stay a few towns away to gain some breathing room (although one collector likened the line of cars heading into town at 4:30 a.m. to "an army convoy"). In the town of Ware, about 20 minutes north of Brimfield, the nine-room (each with a private bath) Wildwood Inn Bed & Breakfast (121 Church St.; 800-860-8098) offers guests a relaxing atmosphere. Sturbridge, a town about 15 miles east of Brimfield, is home to the historic Publick Inn (On the Common; 800-PUBLICK); the 1771 inn's tavern serves up hearty New England fare like fresh seafood and steaming chowders. Clothing or textile collectors shouldn't miss the Antique Textile & Vintage Fashions Extravaganza (Host Hotel, Rte. 20, Sturbridge; 207-439-2334), held 3 times a year on the Monday before Brimfield opens.

Elephant's Trunk Bazaar

NEW MILFORD, CONNECTICUT

Where > Rte. 7, New Milford

When > Sundays March through December, 6:45 a.m. to 2:30 p.m., early-bird 5:45 a.m.

Admission > Early-bird $20, general $1

For more information > (860) 355-1448

With the rolling hills of Litchfield County as a backdrop, 100 to 300 dealers unpack their trucks every Sunday morning, March through December, at the Elephant's Trunk Bazaar. Since its opening in 1977, Elephant's Trunk has become known as the spot in northeastern Connecticut to get your hands on just about anything old and wonderful, including country furniture, architectural salvage, toys, textiles, and luggage. Seasoned attendees say most special here is the element of surprise: Few dealers set up the same types of things every week, so you never know what you're going to find. Trading starts early and ends early and free parking is provided. Pets are banned not only from the sale grounds but also from the parking lot, so leave Fido at home.

It seems fitting that one of the country's best flea markets would be located in an area known both for its natural beauty and its abundance of picturesque New England towns peppered with antiques shops and quiet cafés. For example, about 10 miles from New Milford is the town of Woodbury, dubbed the "Antiques Capital of Connecticut." At least a dozen charming

GUIDE TO THE BEST FLEA MARKETS

shops line Main Street alone, including Country Loft Antiques (557 Main St. S.; 203-266-4500), Joel Einhorn Antiques (452 Main St. S.; 203-266-9090), and Wayne Pratt Antiques (346 Main St. S.; 203-263-5676). Woodbury also boasts a number of memorable lunch spots; two local favorites are the gourmet Good News Café (694 Main St. S.; 203-266-4663) and Mrs. White's Tearoom (308 Sherman Hill Rd.; 203-263-6022).

You'd be hard-pressed to find a more ideal weekend getaway than the shores of Lake Waramaug in New Preston. Lakeside lodging includes the Boulders Inn (387 Lake Rd., Rte. 45; 860-868-0541), an elegant Victorian inn, and the Hopkins Inn (22 Hopkins Rd.; 860-868-7295), a charming farmhouse with a restaurant known for Austrian-inspired specialties like homemade spaetzle, tangy red cabbage, and cinnamon-infused apple strudel. Don't miss a stroll through New Preston's town center, where you'll find a number of quaint shops, such as J. Seitz & Co. (9 E. Shore Rd.; 860-868-0119) and Déjà Vu Antiques (13 Main St.; 860-868-1671).

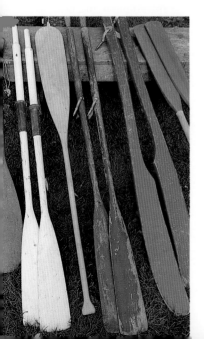

Antiques Week in New Hampshire

MANCHESTER, NEW HAMPSHIRE

Where > Various locations in and around Manchester

When > One week in August, most often the first full week

Admission > Midweek general $10; Bedford Pickers Market Antiques Show early-bird $20, general $6; Deerfield Fairgrounds early-bird $20, general $6; Star of Manchester general $10; Riverside general $8; New Hampshire Antiques Show early-bird $10, general $8

For more information > (845) 876-0616

Ask passionate collectors of classic country antiques if they've got travel plans in August, and a good number will tell you without blinking an eye that they're headed for Manchester, site of the Granite State's annual Antiques Week. Each year, thousands of collectors from across the country and around the world come to enjoy what many call "the antiquing event of the summer." It's an action-packed week to be sure, with six large-scale antiques shows and one major auction of American folk art and furniture, all held in and around the Manchester area. Whether you're looking for pewter chargers and painted cupboards or graniteware mugs and garage sale goodies, there's something here to suit every taste and budget.

It all started back in 1957, when the first New Hampshire Antiques Show was held in two small hotel rooms in the New Hampshire Highway Hotel in Concord. Few of the 17 original exhibitors could have imagined that the show

would spark a weeklong celebration that would still be going strong more than 40 years later. The New Hampshire Antiques Show, sponsored by the New Hampshire Antique Dealers Association, remains the week's cornerstone event, with some 65 dealers offering hand-carved decoys, woven coverlets, Windsor chairs, weather vanes, hooked rugs, and other American treasures. Bargains are found more often at the satellite shows—among them the outdoor Americana Celebration Antiques Show at the Deerfield Fairgrounds and the Bedford Pickers Market Antiques Show at Bedford's Wayfarer Inn—but such finds sometimes require scouring through less spectacular wares.

Accommodations in the Manchester area range from large hotel chains to quaint country bed-and-breakfasts. The Center of New Hampshire Holiday Inn (700 Elm St.; 800-465-4329) hosts the New Hampshire Antiques Show each year, so a room here really puts you in the center of the action. If off the beaten path is more your style, check into the Stillmeadow B & B (545 Main St., Hampstead; 603-329-8381; www.stillmeadowbandb.com), an 1850 Greek Revival about 15 miles southeast of Manchester. Although most of the shows provide food on site, vendors and collectors like to head into town for dinner in one of Manchester's colorful eateries like Richard's Bistro (36 Lowell St.; 603-644-1180) and Shorty's Mexican Roadhouse (1050 Bicentennial Dr.; 603-625-1730).

New England Antiques and Flea Markets, State by State

CONNECTICUT

Antiques in a Cow Pasture

Where > 92 Canaan Rd. (Rte. 44), Salisbury

When > One Saturday in September, 11 a.m. to 4 p.m.,
early-bird 8 a.m.

Admission > Early-bird $20, general $6

For more information > (845) 876-0616; www.barnstar.com

Cheshire Historical Society Antiques & Collectibles Show

Where > 43 Church Dr., Cheshire

When > Last Saturday of the month from April through
October, 9 a.m. to 3 p.m.

Admission > None

For more information > (203) 272-5937

Clinton Village Antique & Collectible Flea Market

Where > 327 E. Main St., Clinton

When > Sundays June through September, 7 a.m. to 4 p.m.

Admission > None

For more information > (860) 669-3839

Coventry Indoor/Outdoor Flea Market

Where > Jct. Rtes. 31 and 275, Coventry

When > Sundays year-round, 9 a.m. to 4 p.m.

Admission > None

For more information > (860) 774-4973

Farmington Antiques Weekend

Where > Farmington Polo Grounds, I-84, exit 39, Farmington

When > Second weekend in June and Labor Day Weekend,
10 a.m. to 5 p.m., early-bird Saturday 7 a.m.

Admission > Early-bird $25, general Saturday $7 and Sunday $5

For more information > (317) 598-0019;
www.farmington-antiques.com

Old Mystic Antique Flea Market

Where > Mystic Visitor and Transportation Center, Old Mystic

When > Sundays year-round 8 a.m. to 5 p.m.

Admission > None

For more information > (860) 536-0646

Woodbury Antiques and Flea Market

Where > Main St., near Jct. Rtes. 6 and 64, Woodbury

When > Saturdays April through November, 5:30 a.m. to 1 p.m.

Admission > None

For more information > (203) 263-2841;
www.woodburyfleamarket.com

MAINE

Hobby Horse Flea Market

Where > Rte. 1, Searsport

When > Weekends May through October, 8 a.m. to 5 p.m.

Admission > None

For more information > (207) 548-2981

Montsweag Flea Market

Where > Rte. 1, Woolwich

When > Wednesdays, Saturdays, and Sundays May through
October, Fridays as well during the summer;
6:30 a.m. to 3 p.m.

Admission > None

For more information > (207) 443-2809

Wiscasset Old Jail Outdoor Antiques Show and Sale

Where > Old Jail, Federal St., Wiscasset

When > Last Saturday of August, 9 a.m. to 3 p.m.

Admission > $4

For more information > (207) 284-8657

Charlton Antique & Flea Market

Where > Trolley Crossings, Rtes. 20 and 31S., Charlton

When > Sunday year-round, Saturdays as well April through November, Saturdays 9 a.m. to 3 p.m., Sundays 7 a.m. to 4 p.m.

Admission > None

For more information > (508) 248-5690

Douglas Flea Market, Antiques, and Collectibles

Where > NE Main St., East Douglas

When > Weekends year-round and holiday Mondays; Saturdays 10 a.m. to 4 p.m., Sundays 8 a.m. to 4 p.m., Mondays 10 a.m. to 2 p.m.

Admission > None

For more information > (508) 278-6027; www.douglasfleamarket.com

Hancock Shaker Village Antiques Show

Where > Round Stone Barn, Rte. 20, Pittsfield

When > One weekend a year, in August, 9:30 a.m. to 5 p.m.

Admission > $6

For more information > (508) 861-5478

Taunton Expo Center Flea Market

Where > 93 Williams St., Taunton

When > Weekends year-round, Saturdays 8 a.m. to 4 p.m., Sundays 7 a.m. to 5 p.m.

Admission > None

For more information > (508) 880-3800

Wellfleet Drive-In Flea Market

Where > Wellfleet Drive-In, 51 Rte. 6, Wellfleet

When > Weekends April through October, Wednesdays and Thursdays in July and August; 8 a.m. to 4 p.m.

Admission > None

For more information > (508) 349-2520

New Hampshire

Amherst Outdoor Antique Market

Where > Rte. 122 S. at the Hollis (N.H.) line, Amherst

When > Last Sunday of the month from April through October, 6 a.m. to 3 p.m.

Admission > None

For more information > (603) 673-2093

Canterbury Shaker Village Antiques Show & Sale

Where > Canterbury Shaker Village, Canterbury

When > Last Saturday in August, 10 a.m. to 4 p.m.

Admission > $10

For more information > (603) 778-8842

Colonial Antiques and Flea Market

Where > Colonial Plaza, I-89, exit 20, West Lebanon

When > Every day, 9 a.m. to 5 p.m.

Admission > None

For more information > (603) 298-7712

Grandview Flea Market

Where > Jct. Rtes. 28 and 28 Bypass, Derry

When > Weekends year-round, 7 a.m. to 3:30 p.m.

Admission > 50¢

For more information > (603) 432-2326

Rhode Island

Big Top Flea Market

Where > 120 Manton Ave., Providence

When > Weekends year-round, 9 a.m. to 5 p.m.

Admission > None

For more information > (401) 274-0060

General Stanton Flea Market

Where > 4115A Old Post Rd., Charleston

When > Weekends April through November, 7 a.m. to 4 p.m.

Admission > None

For more information > (401) 364-8888

Little Compton Antiques Show

Where > Wilbur School, on the Commons, Little Compton

When > First full weekend in August, 10 a.m. to 5 p.m.

Admission > None

For more information > (508) 674-9186

Spring Antiques Show

Where > Providence Country Day School, E. Providence

When > Third weekend in March, Saturday 10 a.m. to 5 p.m.,
Sunday 11 a.m. to 4 p.m.

Admission > None

For more information > (401) 294-2997

Vermont

Charlotte Flea Market

Where > Rte. 7, Charlotte

When > Weekends April through November, 6 a.m. to 5 p.m.

Admission > None

For more information > (802) 425-2844

Manchester Flea Market

Where > Jct. Rtes. 11 and 30, Manchester Center

When > Weekends May through October, 9 a.m. to 5 p.m.

Admission > None

For more information > (802) 362-1631

The Original Newfane Flea Market

Where > Rte. 30, Newfane

When > Sundays May through October, 6 a.m. to 5 p.m.

Admission > None

For more information > (802) 365-4000

Wilmington Outdoor Antique and Flea Market

Where > Jct. Rtes. 9 and 100, Wilmington

When > Weekends and holiday Mondays, Memorial Day
through weekend after Columbus Day, dawn to dusk

Admission > None

For more information > (802) 464-3345

For more listings by state, access www.fleamarketguide.com.

Notes

Use these pages to jot down room dimensions, dealers' phone numbers and specialties, or the address of a noteworthy antiques shop you spot.

_____

_____

_____

_____

_____

_____

_____

_____

_____

_____

_____

_____

_____

_____

_____

_____

_____

Notes

_____

_____

_____

_____

_____

_____

_____

_____

_____

_____

_____

_____

_____

_____

_____

_____

_____

Notes

Middle Atlantic

Where the Sales Are

The Annex Antiques Fair and Flea Market

NEW YORK CITY, NEW YORK

Where > 6th Avenue between 25th and 26th Streets, New York City

When > Weekends year-round, 9 a.m. to 5 p.m.

Admission > $1

For more information > (212) 243-5343

Each Saturday and Sunday throughout the year, a parking lot in the shadow of the Empire State Building is transformed into one of the best treasure-hunting spots in the United States. Manhattan's Annex Antiques Fair and Flea Market, known locally as the 26th Street Flea Market for its main location along 6th Avenue between 25th and 26th Streets, first opened its gates to dealers and collectors in 1976 and now draws several hundred dealers and thousands of eager buyers on a regular basis. Modern furniture from the 1930s through the 1960s is well represented at this sale, as are vintage clothing, linens, and pottery. An abundance of books on antiques, art history, literature, and social customs can also be found. Perhaps most fun, you never know if the person browsing beside you is just an average citizen or a curator at The Metropolitan Museum of Art.

Owing to this market's steady pedestrian traffic over the years, the surrounding streets have become a veritable collector's paradise. A number of large multi-dealerships have sprung up along 25th Street, including the New York Antiques

Center (26 W. 25th St.; 212-337-9600) and the Chelsea Antiques Building (110 W. 25th St.; 212-929-0909). What's more, the Annex itself has two annexes nearby: an outdoor market on the corner of 6th Avenue and 24th Street, and an indoor market known as "The Garage" on 25th Street between 6th and 7th Avenues.

To rest and refuel, try the Antique Café (101 W. 25th St.; 212-675-1663), a cozy neighborhood bistro bustling with shoppers, vendors, and locals. Scrumptious scones, lemon

bars, and cakes as well as savory quiches and pasta salads, make the wait for one of the handful of tables worthwhile. Hotels in the immediate area of the Annex are few and far between, but two nice spots to spend a weekend that are relatively close are the posh W Union Square (201 Park Ave. S.; 212-253-9119) and the more low-key Washington Square Hotel (103 Waverly Pl.; 212-777-9515). Located just off 6th Avenue in the heart of Greenwich Village, the Washington Square Hotel is a quick cab ride from the antiques and flea markets and within walking distance of a downtown enclave of antiques shops along Bleecker Street, on the west side. Peruse quilts and folk art at Susan Parrish Antiques (390 Bleecker St.; 212-645-5020) and colorful, mid-20th-century housewares at Kitschen (17 Perry St.; 212-727-0430). To sample the best cupcakes in town, stop by the Magnolia Bakery (401 Bleecker St.; 212-462-2572).

Lambertville Antiques Market

Where > 1864 River Rd., Lambertville

When > Wednesdays, Saturdays, and Sundays year-round,
6 a.m. to 4 p.m.

Admission > None

For more information > (609) 397-0456

First-time visitors to the Lambertville Antiques Market are sure to notice the wide array of good-quality country antiques and collectibles. But there is something else, something more subtle, that sets this thrice-weekly sale apart from others. Almost everywhere you look, dealers, show managers, and shoppers greet one another and linger to chat like old friends. This tangible sense of community stems in part from the fact that three generations of the Errhalt family have managed the show since it began in 1967. (Beverly Errhalt is the cook at the on-site restaurant, The Market Grill; her homemade soups are legendary.) Two buildings on the premises house single-dealer selections (mainly furniture and other large pieces), and a third building is shared by eight dealers of vintage clothing, jewelry, and various smalls. The remaining vendors set up outside and offer antiques of every description: toy banks, kitchen tins, teacups, Flexible Flyers, and old house shutters, to name just a few.

The town of Lambertville, on the banks of the Delaware River just across from New Hope, PA., is a spot that every antiques enthusiast should visit at least once. Quaint, tree-lined streets harbor dozens of antiques shops, gift boutiques, and home accessory emporiums. Victorian furniture, sterling silver, maps, toys, and pottery fill the 40-dealer cooperative The People's Store Antiques Center (28 N. Union St.; 609-397-9808). The

Blue Raccoon (6 Coryell St.; 609-397-1900), characterized by overstuffed sofas and out-of-the-ordinary accessories, is also home to English bulldogs Dottie and Dash, who stand ready to greet visitors and to accept as much affection as you have time to give. Frothy cappuccinos and substantial muffins make the Lambertville Trading Co. (43 Bridge St.; 609-397-2232) an ideal afternoon pit stop.

Lodging in Lambertville is as unique as the town itself. Many charming bed-and-breakfasts are tucked away on the side streets, including the Bridgestreet House (75 Bridge St.; 800-897-2503), a Federal-style structure with six antiques-filled rooms. The décor of each of the rooms at the Inn at Lambertville Station (11 Bridge St.; 609-397-4400) is inspired by different ports of call: Paris, London, New Orleans, San Francisco, and so on. A renovated 19th-century train depot houses the inn's restaurant and affords diners picturesque views of the Delaware River.

Renninger's Antiques Market

ADAMSTOWN, PENNSYLVANIA

Where > Rte. 272, Adamstown

When > Sundays year-round, 7 a.m. to 4 p.m.

Admission > None

For more information > (877) 336-2177

Dealers who have exhibited at the Renninger's Antiques Market for years report that they have witnessed many a collector gleefully finding the missing piece of a collection that they'd been searching for for ages. It's no wonder: The range of items offered for sale at this Lancaster County market is vast. No matter what you're looking for—fine china, Depression glass, toy trains, paper ephemera, advertising memorabilia, Art Deco furniture—one of Renninger's approximately 375 indoor and 250 outdoor dealers is likely to carry it. In operation since 1967, Renninger's is so renowned, that it's not uncommon to overhear many foreign languages as you wander among the well-stocked booths. "Extravaganzas," held once each in the spring, summer, and fall, tack Saturday onto the regular Sunday-only schedule and often attract additional dealers.

Part of what draws collectors to the Adamstown area is its unusually high concentration of antiques shops, cooperatives, and auctions. The self-proclaimed "Antiques Capital, U.S.A.," Adamstown is also home to Shupp's Grove (Rte. 897 S.; 717-484-4115), a 200- to-300-dealer outdoor flea market, open from late April through October, which focuses on specific areas such as jewelry or kitchen items on designated weekends. The 60-dealer General Heath's Antiques (Jct. Rte. 272 and Stoudtburg Rd.; 717-484-1300) and 300-dealer Stoudtburg Antiques Mall (Rte. 272; 717-484-4385) are also noteworthy.

If you begin to feel tired, experience the restorative quality of hearty Pennsylvania-German fare at Stoudt's Black Angus Steak House & Brew Pub (Rte. 272; 717-484-4385) or Zinn's Diner (Rte. 272, Denver; 717-336-2210). To accommodate the steady stream of antiquers, lodging in the Adamstown area is plentiful. The stately wraparound porch on the Victorian-era Adamstown Inn (62 W. Main St.; 800-594-4808) is an ideal spot to relax after a long day of treasure hunting. About 10 miles southwest of Adamstown is the village of Ephrata, where the Clearview Farm Bed & Breakfast (355 Clearview Rd.; 717-733-6333) sits beside a pond on 200 rolling acres. While in Ephrata, don't miss the Green Dragon Farmer's Market (955 N. State St.; 717-738-1117), held on Fridays. In addition to fresh produce, cheese, and dry goods, this country market also features a vast number of vendors offering antiques and collectibles. The grounds of the Ephrata Cloister (632 W. Main St.; 717-733-6600), a communal society dating back to 1732, are also worth a visit.

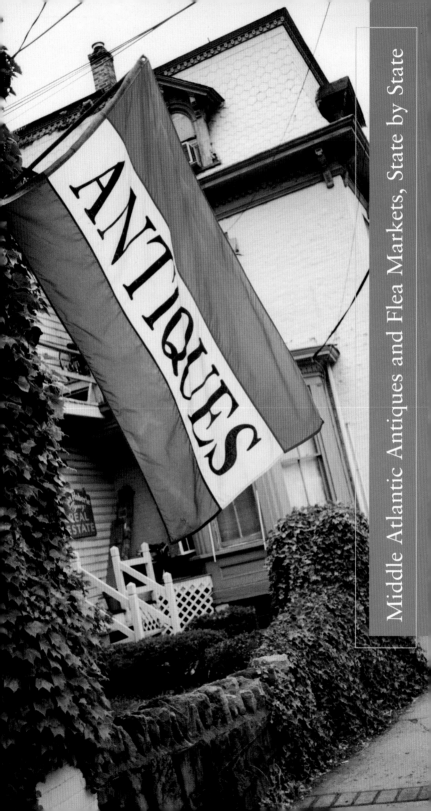

DELAWARE

Bargain Bill Indoor/Outdoor Flea Market

Where > Jct. Rtes. 9-E and 13 Dual, Laurel

When > Friday through Sunday, Fridays 8 a.m. to 4 p.m.,
Saturdays and Sundays year-round 6 a.m. to 5 p.m.

Admission > None

For more information > (302) 875-9958

New Castle Farmers Market

Where > Jct. Rte. 13 and Hares Corner, New Castle

When > Friday through Sunday, Fridays and Saturdays year-round 10 a.m. to 10 p.m., Sundays 10 a.m. to 6 p.m.

Admission > None

For more information > (302) 328-4102

Spence's Auction and Flea Market

Where > 550 S. New St., Dover

When > Tuesdays and Fridays year-round, 8 a.m. to 8 p.m.

Admission > None

For more information > (302) 734-3441

DISTRICT OF COLUMBIA

Capitol Hill Flea Market

Where > Jct. 7th St. and N. Carolina Ave. SE

When > Sundays March to December, 10 a.m. to 5p.m.

Admission > None

For more information > (703) 534-7612

Georgetown Flea Market

Where > Hardy Middle School Parking Lot, Wisconsin Ave. between S and T Sts., Georgetown

When > Sundays year-round, 9 a.m. to 5 p.m.

Admission > None

For more information > (202) 223-0289

MARYLAND

Baltimore Summer Antiques Show

Where > Baltimore Convention Center, Inner Harbor, Baltimore

When > Labor Day weekend and preceding Friday, Friday 12 to 9 p.m., Saturday 11 a.m. to 7 p.m., Sunday 11 a.m. to 5 p.m.

Admission > $10

For more information > (301) 933-9433

Bonnie Brae Flea Market

Where > 1301 Pulaski Hwy., Edgewood

When > Sundays year-round, 7 a.m. to 3 p.m.

Admission > None

For more information > (410) 679-2210

Indian Head Village Green Flea Market

Where > Village Green, Indian Head

When > Saturdays April through October, except Fourth of July, 7 a.m. to 1 p.m.

Admission > None

For more information > (301) 743-5574

North Point Drive-In Indoor/Outdoor Flea Market

Where > 4001 N. Point Blvd., Baltimore

When > Weekends year-round, 7 a.m. to 2 p.m.

Admission > None

For more information > (410) 477-1337

The Columbia Market

Where > Rte. 175, Columbia

When > Sundays end of April through October, 8 a.m. to 3 p.m.

Admission > None

For more information > (410) 679-2288

NEW JERSEY

Atlantique City

Where > Atlantic City Convention Center, Atlantic City

When > Fourth weekend in March and third weekend in October, Saturdays 10 a.m. to 8 p.m., Sundays 10 a.m. to 5 p.m.

Admission > Saturday $15, Sunday $10; purchase in advance for both days $24

For more information > (609) 926-1800; www.atlantiquecity.com

Columbus Farmer's Market

Where > 2919 Rte. 206 S., Columbus

When > Thursday, Saturday, and Sunday year-round, dawn to 1:30 p.m.

Admission > None

For more information > (609) 267-0400

Englishtown Auction Flea Market

Where > 90 Wilson Ave., Englishtown

When > Weekends year-round, Saturdays 7 a.m. to 4 p.m., Sundays 9 a.m. to 4 p.m.

Admission > None

For more information > (732) 446-9644

Flemington Fair Flea Market

Where > Hwy. 31, Flemington

When > Wednesdays April through October, 6 a.m. to 4 p.m.

Admission > None

For more information > (908) 782-7326

Manahawkin Flea Market

Where > 657 E. Bay Ave., Manahawkin

When > Friday through Sunday year-round, Fridays and
Saturdays, 9 a.m. to 5 p.m., Sundays 9 a.m. to 4 p.m.

Admission > None

For more information > (609) 597-1017

Ocean Grove Flea Market

Where > Stretching from the Great Auditorium to the
boardwalk, Ocean Grove

When > First Saturday after Memorial Day and first Saturday
after Labor Day, 9 a.m. to 4 p.m.

Admission > None

For more information > (732) 774-1391

NEW YORK

Antiques and Crafts Market

Where > Historic Richmond Town, Staten Island

When > First Sunday in June, Sunday after Labor Day,
and first Sunday in October, 10 a.m. to 5 p.m.

Admission > None

For more information > (718) 351-1611

Heart of the Village Antiques Fair

Where > First Presbyterian Church, East Hampton

When > Second Friday and Saturday in June, Fourth of July weekend, and first weekend in August; 10 a.m. to 5 p.m., early-bird Friday 9 to 10 a.m.

Admission > Early-bird $8, general $5

For more information > (631) 324-6893

Madison-Bouckville Outdoor Antiques Show

Where > Rte. 20, Bouckville

When > Third weekend in August, early-bird Friday 10 a.m., Saturday and Sunday 9 a.m. to 5 p.m.

Admission > Early-bird Friday $40, general $5

For more information > (315) 824-2462; www.bouckvilleantiqueshow.com

Rhinebeck Antiques Fair

Where > Dutchess County Fairgrounds, Rhinebeck

When > Three weekends a year, in May, July, and October; Saturdays 10 a.m. to 5 p.m., Sundays 11 a.m. to 4 p.m. July Saturday 9 a.m. to 5 p.m.

Admission > May and October shows $7, July show $6

For more information > (845) 876-1989

Stormville Airport Antique Show and Flea Market

Where > Rte. 216, Stormville

When > Weekends of Memorial Day, Fourth of July, Labor Day, and Columbus Day, last Sunday in April, and first Sunday in August and November; dawn to dusk

Admission > None

For more information > (845) 221-6561

Triple Pier Expo

Where > Passenger Ship Piers 88, 90, and 92, New York City

When > Two weekends in March and two weekends in November, Saturday 9 a.m. to 6 p.m., Sunday 11 a.m. to 7 p.m.

Admission > $12

For more information > (212) 255-0020

PENNSYLVANIA

Collector's Cove

Where > Jct. Rtes. 33 and 209, Sciota

When > Saturdays and Sundays year-round, 9 a.m. to 5 p.m.

Admission > None

For more information > (570) 992-5110;
www.covemarket.com

Greengate Outdoor Flea Market

Where > Rte. 30, Greensburg

When > Sundays, year-round, outdoors April through October, 7 a.m. to 3 p.m.

Admission > None

For more information > (724) 837-6881

Quaker City Flea Market

Where > Jct. Tacony and Comly Sts., Philadelphia

When > Weekends year-round, 8 a.m. to 4 p.m.

Admission > None

For more information > (215) 744-2022

Renninger's Antique Market #2

Where > 740 Nobel St., Kutztown

When > Saturdays year-round, 8 a.m. to 5 p.m.

Admission > None

For more information > (610) 683-6848

Shupp's Grove

Where > Rte. 897S, Adamstown

When > Weekends late April through October, 7 a.m. to 5 p.m.

Admission > None

For more information > (717) 484-4115

Silver Spring Flea Market

Where > 6416 Carlisle Pike, Mechanicsburg

When > Sundays, 6 a.m. to 3 p.m.

Admission > None

For more information > (717) 766-7215

SuperFlea Flea Market

Where > 833 E. Pittsburgh-McKeesport Blvd., Pittsburgh

When > Weekends, 8 a.m. to 4 p.m.

Admission > None

For more information > (412) 673-3532

For more listings by state, access www.fleamarketguide.com.

Notes

Use these pages to jot down room dimensions, dealers' phone numbers
and specialties, or the address of a noteworthy antiques shop you spot.

_____

_____

_____

_____

_____

_____

_____

_____

_____

_____

_____

_____

_____

_____

_____

_____

_____

Notes

_____

_____

_____

_____

_____

_____

_____

_____

_____

_____

_____

_____

_____

_____

_____

_____

_____

_____

Notes

_____

_____

_____

_____

_____

_____

_____

_____

_____

_____

_____

_____

_____

_____

_____

_____

_____

_____

_____

Notes

_____

_____

_____

_____

_____

_____

_____

_____

_____

_____

_____

_____

_____

_____

_____

_____

_____

_____

South

Where the Sales Are

Lakewood Antiques Market

ATLANTA, GEORGIA

Where > Lakewood Fairgrounds, Atlanta

When > Second weekend and preceding Friday of every month, Fridays and Saturdays 9 a.m. to 6 p.m., Sundays 10 a.m. to 5 p.m., early-bird Thursdays 3 p.m.

Admission > Early-bird $4, general $3

For more information > (404) 622-4488; www.lakewoodantiques.com

Come the second weekend of each month, many Southern collectors and antiques dealers pack up their cars and make their way toward Atlanta. Their destination is the Lakewood Fairgrounds, where the Lakewood Antiques Market is held. One devoted fan described the sale in these simple terms: lots of smiling people and lots of great stuff. The sale is large—some 1,300 to 1,500 vendors occupy five buildings, two open sheds, and two courtyards—and lively. A low buzz permeates all corners of the market, as shoppers negotiate prices for printed tablecloths, painted cupboards, iron beds, Fire-King dinnerware, vintage lighting fixtures, Pez dispensers, homespun textiles, and fanciful hats and clothing. The buzz continues around the concession carts—where fresh doughnuts, corn dogs, and refreshing iced tea are favorites—as friends swap stories of their fun finds.

Still have some energy? After spending the morning scouring the booths at Lakewood, many shoppers delay their

trip home and instead head across town to another of Atlanta's premier antiques markets: Scott's, held on the same weekend at the Atlanta Exposition Center. Here you will find an even larger number of vendors, more than 2,000 in all, filling Expo North and Expo South (shuttle buses connect the two sites) as well as open-air areas, weather permitting. Scott's feels a bit more formal than Lakewood—decorators often frequent Scott's when searching for fine furniture, Turkish carpets, sterling silver, lush brocades and damasks, bronze statuary, and the like.

For an enjoyable afternoon stroll, head to Atlanta's Virginia-Highland district, a neighborhood brimming with shops and cafés. Foxgloves and Ivy Florist (1058 St. Charles Ave.; 404-892-7272) harbors a small selection of garden antiques for those looking to find pieces for their outdoor areas. Anyone seeking furniture and accessories from the 1930s through the 1960s should stop by 20th Century Antiques (1044 N. Highland Ave.; 404-892-2065). Good bets when you're hungry include Aurora Coffee (992 N. Highland Ave.; 404-607-1300) and, for dinner, Dish (870 N. Highland Ave.; 404-897-3463). Within Virginia-Highland, the 1913 Craftsman-style Gaslight Inn (1001 St. Charles Ave.; 404-875-1001) welcomes guests with seven antique-filled rooms. Another gracious Atlanta establishment is the Shellmont Inn (821 Piedmont Ave.; 404-872-9290), a restored 1891 Victorian building surrounded by a bountiful garden.

Metrolina Exposition Antiques & Antique Collectibles Market

CHARLOTTE, NORTH CAROLINA

Where > 7100 Statesville Rd., Charlotte

When > First weekend and preceding Friday of every month based on the first Saturday of the month, Fridays and Saturdays 8 a.m. to 5 p.m., Sundays 9 a.m. to 5 p.m., early-bird Thursdays 8 a.m. to 5 p.m.; April, June, and November Spectaculars, Thursdays 8 a.m. to 5 p.m., early-bird Wednesdays 9 a.m. to 5 p.m.

Admission > Early-bird $10, general $4; April and November Spectaculars early-bird $50, general $6; June Spectacular early-bird $35, general $6

For more information > (800) 824-3770; www.metrolinaexpo.com

There are flea markets and antique fairs you can see in a day, and then there's the Metrolina Expo Antiques & Antique Collectibles Market. Held on the first full weekend of every month and the Friday preceding it, this show regularly attracts some 1,500 dealers who occupy 20 buildings and, from April through November, dozens of outdoor tents as well. During "Spectacular" shows in April, June, and November, the number of vendors swells to a staggering 6,000. These shows begin on Thursday, but early-birds can get in on Wednesday. If you're looking for Victorian furniture, Southern folk pottery, Coca-Cola memorabilia, clocks, or records, this sale is worth your while.

When locals crave an afternoon of antiquing and strolling from one treasure-filled shop to the next, they often head to Waxhaw, a small town located about 15 miles south of Charlotte. More than two dozen antiques stores, home design emporiums, and cafés populate Waxhaw's historic district, including Red Barn Gallery Antiques (103 S. Church St.; 704-843-1309), a repository of country furniture, pottery, glassware, toys, and a large number of dolls. Five dealers share space at Junction

Antiques (100 E. South Main St.; 704-843-3350) and display a wonderful selection of china, textiles, kitchenware, and one-of-a-kind items. Waxhaw eateries range from coffee shops ideal for a quick stop to elegant bistros like Dearstyne's (116 W. North Main St.; 704-243-2090), which features Sunday brunch, served from 11 a.m. to 2 p.m., and always draws a crowd.

For a bustling city, Charlotte boasts a number of charming country inns, like the quaint Homeplace Bed & Breakfast (5901 Sardis Rd.; 704-365-1936). Visitors to this restored 1902 dwelling can relax on the wide wraparound porch or navigate the brick paths through gracious gardens on the property's two and a half wooded acres. Lovers of antiques will also enjoy the Morehead Inn (1122 E. Morehead St.; 888-MOREHEAD), an elegant 1917 residence in one of Charlotte's oldest neighborhoods. Here, guests can stay in the main house or in a carriage house overlooking a secluded courtyard.

Antiques Week in Round Top

Where > Various locations in and around Round Top

When > Twice a year, Tuesday through Sunday of the first full week of April and October. Round Top Antiques Fair Saturday 9 a.m. to 6 p.m., Sunday 9 a.m. to 4 p.m.; Marburger Farm Antique Show early-bird Tuesday 10 a.m. to 2 p.m., general Tuesday 2 to 5 p.m., Wednesday through Saturday 9 a.m. to 5 p.m.

Admission > Round Top Antiques Fair $10, Marburger Farm Antique Show early-bird $15, general $5

For more information > Round Top Antiques Fair, (281) 493-5501, www.roundtopantiquesfair.com; Marburger Farm Antique Show, (800) 947-5799, www.roundtop-marburger.com

Twice a year, in April and October, collectors come from far and wide to hunt for treasures in the tiny Texas town of Round Top, population 81. Local visionary Emma Lee Turney is credited with putting this sleepy hamlet—located along the main highway connecting Austin and Houston—on the map. It was back in the late 1960s that Turney organized the first Round Top Antiques Fair. Both the crowds and the press coverage grew with each passing year, and eventually a weeklong celebration of American country antiques was born. Turney's show remains the jewel in the crown: The three-day (Friday, Saturday, and Sunday), four-location event boasts more than 400 dealers. And even though the high-quality items and sometimes substantial price tags will let you know right away that this is

no "flea market," all visitors to Round Top should still stroll through this show at least once to see the best of the best.

Sleepers and more affordable items are to be found at the satellite shows that have sprung up in and around Round Top. Among the biggest is the Marburger Farm Antique Show (Tuesday through Saturday). Under the sprawling Texas sky, Marburger's cluster of large and small tents houses some 350 dealers displaying their selections of painted furniture, Indian trade blankets, enamelware, advertising memorabilia, yellowware, quilts, and more. Although this show is still in its infancy—it started in 1997—it's already garnered a loyal following. Another spot that savvy collectors comb is nearby Warrenton, which literally transforms into a townwide antiques sale. Yard sale signs are found at every crossroad and dance hall tables overflow with dealers' wares.

Aside from the great antiques and collectibles to be found, the thing that Round Top regulars look forward to most is a return trip to Royers' Round Top Café (105 Main St.; 979-249-3611). The wait for a table might be long, but during Antiques Week you can make a reservation. The menu includes mouthwatering steaks, seafood, pasta, and Royers's famous homemade pies—pecan, chocolate chip, and cherry to name just a few. Charming country inns nestled amid towering oak trees surround Round Top, including the three-room Anderson's Round Top Inn (102 Bauer-Rummel Rd.; 979-249-5294) and the Heart of My Heart Ranch (Florida Chapel Rd.; 800-327-1242), where gourmet breakfasts are served on a wide porch overlooking a pond.

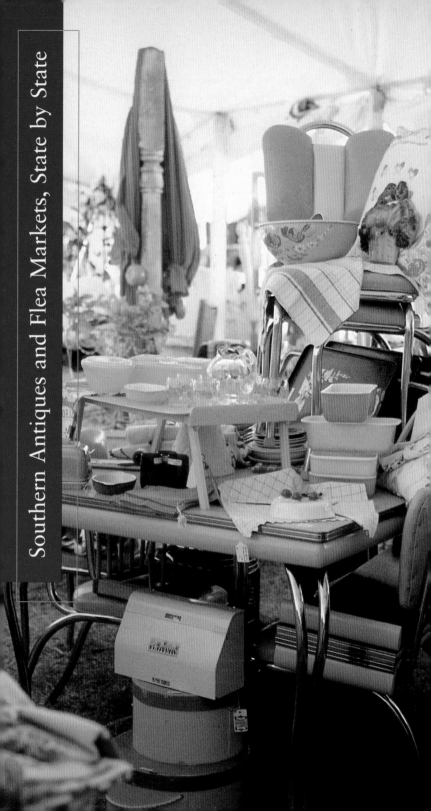

Southern Antiques and Flea Markets, State by State

ALABAMA

Birmingham Fairgrounds Flea Market

Where > Alabama State Fairgrounds, Birmingham

When > First weekend and preceding Friday of every month and first three weekends and preceding Fridays in December; Fridays 3 to 7 p.m., Saturdays 9 a.m. to 6 p.m, Sundays 9 a.m. to 5 p.m.

Admission > None

For more information > (800) 3-MARKET

Collinsville Trade Day

Where > Hwy. 11 S., Collinsville

When > Saturdays, dawn to 2:30 p.m.

Admission > 50¢

For more information > (256) 524-2127

Cullman Flea Market

Where > 415 Lincoln Ave. SW, Cullman

When > Weekends year-round, 8 a.m. to 5 p.m.

Admission > None

For more information > (256) 739-0910

First Monday Flea Market

Where > Courthouse Square, Scottsboro

When > First Monday and preceding Sunday of every month, 8 a.m. to dusk

Admission > None

For more information > (256) 574-4468; www.firstmonday.com

Flea Market Mobile

Where > 401 Schillings Rd. N., Mobile

When > Weekends year-round, 9 a.m. to 5 p.m.

Admission > None

For more information > (334) 633-7533; www.fleamarketmobile.com

World's Longest Yard Sale—450 Miles

Where > 450-mile yard sale stretching north from Gadsden into Tennessee and Kentucky

When > Four days in August, dawn to dusk

Admission > None

For more information > (256) 549-0351; www.127sale.com

ARKANSAS

Daisies & Olives Antiques & Gifts

Where > 129-135 E. Buchanan St., Prairie Grove

When > Every day year-round, Mondays through Saturdays 9 a.m. to 5 p.m., Sundays 10 a.m. to 5 p.m.

Admission > None

For more information > (501) 846-1800

Higdon Ferry Flea Market

Where > 2138 Higdon Ferry Rd., Hot Springs

When > Every day year-round, 10 a.m. to 5 p.m.

Admission > None

For more information > (501) 525-9927

Memphis Flea Market

Where > Little Rock Exposition Center, 13000 I-30, Little Rock

When > Second weekend of every month, 8 a.m. to 6 p.m.

Admission > $1

For more information > (501) 455-1001

Thackerland Flea Market

Where > 666 Hwy. 367, Judsonia

When > Daily, 10 a.m. to 5 p.m.

Admission > None

For more information > (501) 729-3063

FLORIDA

Beach Boulevard Flea Market

Where > 11041 Beach Blvd., Jacksonville

When > Weekends year-round, 7 a.m. to 6 p.m.

Admission > None

For more information > (904) 645-5961

Florida Twin Markets

Where > Hwy. 441, Mt. Dora

When > Weekends year-round with three-day extravaganzas in November, January, and February, 9 a.m. to 5 p.m.

Admission > None

For more information > (352) 383-8393

Key Largo Warehouse Market

Where > U.S. Rte. 1, Key Largo

When > Weekends, 7 a.m. to 5 p.m.

Admission > None

For more information > (305) 451-0677

Naples Drive-In Flea Market

Where > 7700 E. Davis Blvd., Naples

When > Weekends, 7 a.m. to 3 p.m., plus Fridays October through April 7 a.m. to 3 p.m.

Admission > None

For more information > (941) 774-2900

Piccadilly Antique and Collectible Fair

Where > South Florida Fairgrounds, West Palm Beach

When > Usually the first weekend of every month, Saturdays 9 a.m. to 5 p.m., Sundays 10 a.m. to 4:30 p.m., early-bird Fridays 12 to 5 p.m.

Admission > Early-bird $10, general $6

For more information > (727) 345-4431; www.piccadillypromos.com

Three Star Flea Market

Where > 2390 S. Orange Blossom Tr., Apopka

When > Weekends year-round, dawn to dusk

Admission > None

For more information > (407) 293-2722

Webster Westside Flea Market

Where > Jct. Hwy. 478 and NW 3rd St., Webster

When > Mondays year-round, 5 a.m. to dusk

Admission > None

For more information > (800) 832-7396

GEORGIA

Flowery Branch Antique Market

Where > 5540 Atlanta Hwy., Flowery Branch

When > First full weekend and preceding Friday of every month, Fridays and Saturdays 9 a.m. to 6 p.m., Sundays 9 a.m. to 4 p.m.

Admission > None

For more information > (770) 967-9080

Keller's Flea Market

Where > 5901 Ogeechee Rd., Savannah

When > Weekends year-round, 8 a.m. to 6 p.m.

Admission > None

For more information > (912) 927-4848

Kudzu Antiques

Where > 2874 E. Ponce de Leon, Decatur

When > Friday through Sunday, Fridays and Saturdays 10:30 a.m. to 5:30 p.m., Sundays 12:30 to 5:30 p.m.

Admission > None

For more information > (404) 373-6498

Lake Acworth Antique and Flea Market

Where > 4375 Cobb Pkwy. NW, Acworth

When > Weekends year-round, 7 a.m. to 5 p.m.

Admission > None

For more information > (770) 974-5896

Scotts Antique Market Show

Where > Atlanta Exposition Center, Atlanta

When > Second weekend and preceding Friday of every month, Fridays and Saturdays 9 a.m. to 6 p.m., Sundays 10 a.m. to 4 p.m.

Admission > $3

For more information > (740) 569-4112

KENTUCKY

Kentucky Flea Market

Where > Kentucky Fair and Exposition Center, Louisville

When > Various weekends, including preceding Friday, February through December; Friday 12 to 7 p.m., Saturday 10 a.m. to 7 p.m., Sunday 11 a.m. to 5 p.m.

Admission > None

For more information > (502) 456-2244; www.stewartpromotions.com

Old-Fashioned Court Days

Where > Various sites around the town, Maysville

When > First weekend of October, 9 a.m. to 10 p.m.

Admission > None

For more information > (606) 564-9419

Richwood Flea Market

Where > 10915 U.S. Rte. 25, Richwood

When > Tuesdays, Saturdays, and Sundays year-round; Tuesdays dawn to 1 p.m., Saturdays and Sundays 9 a.m. to 5 p.m.

Admission > None

For more information > (859) 371-5800

Shelby County Flea Market

Where > 820 Buck Creek Rd., Simpsonville

When > Weekends year-round, 9 a.m. to 5 p.m.

Admission > None

For more information > (502) 722-8883

World's Longest Yard Sale—450 Miles

Where > 450-mile yard sale stretching south from Covington through Tennessee and Alabama

When > Four days in August, dawn to dusk

Admission > None

For more information > (502) 564-4890; www.127sale.com

LOUISIANA

Community Flea Market

Where > French Market, 1200 block of N. Peters St., New Orleans

When > Every day, 7 a.m. to 7 p.m.

Admission > None

For more information > (504) 596-3420

Deep South Flea Market

Where > 5905 Florida Blvd., Baton Rouge

When > Fridays, Saturdays, and Sundays year-round, 10 a.m. to 6 p.m.

Admission > None

For more information > (225) 923-0333

Greenwood Flea Market

Where > 9249 Jefferson-Paige Rd., Greenwood

When > Weekends year-round, 9 a.m. to 6 p.m.

Admission > None

For more information > (318) 938-7201

Jefferson Flea Market

Where > 2134 Airline Dr., Kenner

When > Fridays, Saturdays, and Sundays year-round, 10 a.m. to 6 p.m.

Admission > None

For more information > (504) 461-0128

MISSISSIPPI

Fairgrounds Antique Flea Market

Where > 900 High St., Jackson

When > Weekends year-round, Saturdays 8 a.m. to 5 p.m., Sundays 10 a.m. to 5 p.m.

Admission > None

For more information > (601) 353-5327

North Carolina

Fairgrounds Flea Market

Where > North Carolina State Fairgrounds, Jct. Blue Ridge Rd. and Hillsboro St., Raleigh

When > Weekends November through September, 9 a.m. to 5 p.m.

Admission > None

For more information > (919) 829-3533

Jamestown Flea and Farmer's Market

Where > Jamestown Rd., Morgantown

When > Fridays, Saturdays, Sundays year-round, 7 a.m. to 5 p.m.

Admission > None

For more information > (828) 584-4038

Smiley's Flea Market

Where > Hwy. 25, Fletcher

When > Fridays, Saturdays, and Sundays year-round, 7 a.m. to 5 p.m.

Admission > None

For more information > (828) 684-3532

Springs Road Flea Market

Where > 3451 Springs Rd., Hickory

When > Weekends year-round, 8 a.m. to 4 p.m.

Admission > None

For more information > (828) 256-7669

Starway Flea Market

Where > 2346 Carolina Beach Rd., Wilmington

When > Friday through Sunday year-round, Fridays and Sundays 7:30 a.m. to 4 p.m., Saturdays 6 a.m. to 4 p.m.

Admission > 50¢

For more information > (910) 763-5520

South Carolina

Barnyard Flea Market

Where > Rte. 1, Lexington

When > Fridays, Saturdays, and Sundays year-round, dawn to dusk

Admission > None

For more information > (800) 628-7496

Coastal Carolina Flea Market

Where > Jct. Hwy. 78 and College Park Rd., Ladson

When > Weekends year-round, 8 a.m. to 5 p.m.

Admission > None

For more information > (843) 797-0540

Lowcountry Market

Where > Gaillard Auditorium, 77 Calhoun St., Charleston

When > Usually the third weekend of every month, Saturdays 9 a.m. to 6 p.m., Sundays 10 a.m. to 5 p.m.

Admission > $2

For more information > (843) 849-1949

Myrtle Beach Flea Market

Where > 3820 S. Kings Hwy., Myrtle Beach

When > Thursdays, Fridays, Saturdays, and Sundays, September through May; every day Memorial Day through Labor Day, 9 a.m. to 6 p.m.

Admission > None

For more information > (843) 477-1550

Springfield Flea Market

Where > 9113 Neeses Hwy., Springfield

When > Saturdays and Mondays year-round, dawn to 2 p.m.

Admission > None

For more information > (803) 258-3192

TENNESSEE

Esau's Antique and Collectible Market

Where > Chilhowee Park, Knoxville

When > Third weekend of every month, Saturdays 9 a.m. to 5 p.m., Sundays 12 to 5 p.m.

Admission > $3

For more information > (800) 588-ESAU; www.esaushows.com

First Monday Flea Market

Where > Gibson County Fairgrounds, Trenton

When > First Monday and preceding weekend of every month, 6 a.m. to dusk

Admission > None

For more information > (901) 855-2981; www.firstmonday.com

Flea Market at the Nashville Fairgrounds

Where > Tennessee State Fairgrounds, Nashville

When > Fourth weekend of every month except December, Saturdays 6 a.m. to 6 p.m., Sundays 7 a.m. to 4 p.m.

Admission > None

For more information > (615) 862-5016

Great Smokies Flea Market

Where > 220 Dumplin Valley Rd., Kodak

When > Fridays, Saturdays, and Sundays year-round, 9 a.m. to 6 p.m.

Admission > None

For more information > (865) 932-3532

Memphis Flea Market

Where > Mid-South Fairgrounds, Memphis

When > Third weekend of every month, 8 a.m. to 6 p.m.

Admission > None

For more information > (901) 276-3532;
www.memphisfleamarket.com

World's Longest Yard Sale—450 Miles

Where > 450-mile yard sale bisecting the state and continuing
north and south into Kentucky and Alabama

When > Four days in August, dawn to dusk

Admission > None

For more information > (800) 327-3945; www.127sale.com

TEXAS

Austin Country Flea Market

Where > 9500 Hwy. 290, Austin

When > Weekends year-round, 10 a.m. to 6 p.m.

Admission > None

For more information > (512) 928-2795

Buchanan's Antiques and Collectibles Flea Market

Where > Automobile Building of Dallas Fair Park, Dallas

When > One weekend a month year-round, 9 a.m. to 5 p.m.,
early-bird Fridays 10 a.m. to 7 p.m.

Admission > Early-bird $10, general $3

For more information > (405) 478-4050

First Monday Trade Days

Where > Hwy. 19, Canton

When > Thursday through Sunday preceding the first Monday of every month, dawn to dusk

Admission > None

For more information > (903) 567-6556;
www.firstmonday.com

Mission Open-Air Flea Market

Where > 207 W. Chavaneaux Rd., San Antonio

When > Wednesdays, Saturdays, and Sundays year-round, 6 a.m. to 4 p.m.

Admission > None

For more information > (210) 923-8131

Third Monday Trade Days

Where > Hwy. 380, McKinney

When > Weekend preceding the third Monday of every month, 9 a.m. to 4 p.m.

Admission > None

For more information > (972) 562-5466

Weatherford Trade Days

Where > Jct. Santa Fe Dr. and Ft. Worth Hwy., Weatherford

When > Friday through Sunday preceding the first Monday of every month, dawn to dusk

Admission > None

For more information > (817) 594-3801;
www.firstmonday.com

Virginia

Bellwood Flea Market

Where > 9201 Jefferson Davis Hwy., Richmond

When > Weekends year-round, 5:30 a.m. to 4:30 p.m.

Admission > None

For more information > (800) 793-0707

D.C. Big Flea

Where > Chantilly Shopping Center, Chantilly

When > Various weekends year-round, Saturdays 10 a.m.
to 6 p.m., Sundays 11 a.m. to 5 p.m.

Admission > $5

For more information > (757) 430-4735;
www.bigfleamarket.com

Manor Mart Flea Market

Where > Hwy. 1, Fredericksburg

When > Weekends year-round, dawn to dusk

Admission > None

For more information > (540) 898-4685

Norfolk Flea Market

Where > 3416 N. Military Hwy., Norfolk

When > Weekends year-round, dawn to dusk

Admission > None

For more information > (757) 857-7824

Richmond Big Flea

Where > Richmond Raceway Complex, 600 E. Laburnum Ave.,
Richmond

When > Various weekends year-round, Saturdays 10 a.m. to
6 p.m., Sundays 12 to 5 p.m.

Admission > $3

For more information > (757) 430-4735;
www.bigfleamarket.com

WEST VIRGINIA

Harpers Ferry Flea Market

Where > Jct. Hwy. 340 and Bloomery Rd., Harpers Ferry

When > Weekends March through November, dawn to dusk

Admission > None

For more information > (304) 725-4141;
www.harpersferryfleamkt.com

I-81 Flea Market

Where > Exit 20 off I-81, Martinsburg

When > Fridays, Saturdays, and Sundays year-round,
7 a.m. to 5 p.m.

Admission > None

For more information > (304) 274-3387

Milton Flea Market

Where > Rte. 60, Milton

When > Friday through Sunday year-round, Fridays 8 a.m.
to 4 p.m., Saturdays and Sundays 8 a.m. to 5 p.m.

Admission > None

For more information > (304) 743-1123

For more listings by state, access www.fleamarketguide.com.

Notes

Use these pages to jot down room dimensions, dealers' phone numbers and specialties, or the address of a noteworthy antiques shop you spot.

_____

_____

_____

_____

_____

_____

_____

_____

_____

_____

_____

_____

_____

_____

_____

_____

_____

_____

Notes

Notes

Midwest

Where the Sales Are

Collector's Paradise
Flea Market

Where > Keokuk County Fairgrounds, What Cheer

When > First Sunday and preceding Saturday in May, August, and
October, 7 a.m. to dusk

Admission > $1

For more information > (641) 634-2109

What Cheer is a small farm town in Iowa, approximately
equidistant from the larger cities of Des Moines and Cedar
Rapids. But "what cheer" might just as easily be used to describe
the reaction of collectors who attend the thrice-annual flea
market that's been held at the Keokuk County Fairgrounds for
more than 20 years. Aptly named Collector's Paradise, this
sale averages 300 to 500 vendors and is a veritable treasure
trove of classic country antiques and collectibles. Kitchenware is
out in force—advertising tins, mixing bowls, salt and pepper
shakers, whisks, wire baskets, and those desirable table-and-chair
sets from the 1950s—as are painted cupboards, trading cards,
Depression glass, vintage bicycles, and much, much more.

The countryside surrounding What Cheer is ideal for
leisurely rambles. Long stretches of cornfields are broken up
by creeks and glens, and throughout, small towns harbor
wonderful surprises—whether it is a top-notch sandwich shop,
a world-class quilt museum, or a Main Street that looks as if it
belongs in a movie. Descendants of the Dutch settlers of Pella,

a town about 30 miles west of What Cheer, have created a little bit of Holland right here, with windmills, acres of tulips, and a 21-building Historical Village (507 Franklin St.; 641-628-4311). Pella's Strawtown Inn (1111 Washington St.; 641-621-9500) is listed on the National Register of Historic Places and is a quiet place to rest and revive.

Kalona, a town about 30 miles east of What Cheer, boasts one of the area's hidden gems, the Kalona Quilt and Textile Museum (515 B Ave.; 319-656-3232), which is housed in the Kalona Historical Village. The museum's collection spans three centuries and features a fantastic selection of quilts from the region's thriving Amish community. About 15 miles northeast of Kalona, the Sheraton Iowa City (210 S. Dubuque St.; 800-848-1335) serves as a good base of operations from which to explore the entire area. Another worthwhile stop is the Amana Colonies, about 20 miles northwest of Iowa City, where you will find a wide array of quaint shops. A number of cafés, restaurants, book and gift shops, and occasionally live music in the evenings can be found nearby on the lively Iowa City pedestrian mall.

Springfield Antique Show and Flea Market

SPRINGFIELD, OHIO

Where > Clark County Fairgrounds, Springfield

When > Third weekend and preceding Friday of every month,
Fridays 5 to 8 p.m., Saturdays 8 a.m. to 5 p.m.,
Sundays 9 a.m. to 4 p.m. Early-bird Friday before 12 p.m.

Admission > Early-bird $10, general $2

For more information > (937) 325-0053

For more than a quarter century, Ohio antiquers have dedicated the third weekend and preceding Friday of the month to combing the Springfield Antique Show and Flea Market for castoffs and collectibles. This sizable indoor/outdoor sale attracts approximately 500 dealers in the winter and about 1,000 in the warmer months. Then there are "Extravaganzas"—held three times a year, in the spring, summer, and fall—which average about 2,000 to 3,000 vendors and are always well attended by local collectors. Regulars have come to expect an eclectic mix: Old tools and farm equipment might be found next to a late-1800s toaster that sits atop a jewelry box filled with beaded baubles from the 1960s. What's more, this sale's central-Ohio location makes it a great place to hunt for pottery by some of the state's best-known manufacturers, including Roseville and McCoy.

Springfield is also home to a number of large multi-dealerships that are worth a visit. More than 200 dealers are represented in the AAA I-70 Antique Mall (4700 S. Charleston Pike; 937-324-8448), and the Heart of Ohio Antique Center (4785 E. National Rd.; 937-324-2188) showcases the wares of about 650 dealers. The town has become such a mecca for collectors that one local hotel, the Springfield Inn (100 S. Fountain Ave.; 800-234-3611), offers discounts to guests who come to town just to go antiquing.

Although Springfield has much to entice the collector, visitors should also take the opportunity to explore some of the small towns in the surrounding countryside. The town of Clifton, about five miles south of Springfield, is home to the Clifton Antique Mall (301 N. Main St.; 937-767-2277) and an 1802 gristmill that is still in operation. Old Clifton Days offers a townwide yard sale among the other festivities during the weekend after Labor Day. Also worth a visit is the nearby village of Yellow Springs, a thriving crafts community. Glassblowers, doll makers, potters, jewelry designers, and photographers all call this charming town home. Favorite local eateries include the Winds Café (215 Xenia Ave.; 937-767-1144) and Young's Jersey Dairy (6880 Springfield-Xenia Rd.; 937-325-0629), a working dairy farm whose gift shop will be of special interest to collectors of cow memorabilia. Accommodations at a local country bed and breakfast, like S. Charleston's Houstonia Bed and Breakfast (25 E. Mound St.; 888-462-8855), put you in the center of all that the Springfield area has to offer.

Third Sunday Market

Where > McClean County Fairgrounds, Interstate Center, Bloomington

When > Third Sunday of the month from May through October, early-bird 6:30 a.m., general 8 a.m. to 4 p.m.

Admission > Early-bird $25, general $5

For more information > (800) 433-8226

From May through October, many Midwestern collectors clear their calendars to accommodate the Third Sunday Market, a flea market devoted exclusively to antiques and collectibles. Held at the McClean County Fairgrounds since the late 1980s, this indoor/outdoor sale features more than 400 dealers. Whether you're looking for Fiestaware or finely carved mahogany furniture, you're likely to find it here. Excitement is in the air when the market opens, as collectors rush through to see what new objects the dealers have discovered in the weeks since the last show. Many vendors report that they scour the countryside and often travel to other states to find great things, then bring them to Bloomington, where they are eagerly scooped up by collectors. Old playthings can be found in abundance, including pedal cars, vintage Barbie dolls, board games, and die-cast racing cars.

If spending the weekend in town, collectors will find numerous shops and attractions to keep them busy. At the top of the list is the Bloomington Antique Mall (102 N. Center St.; 309-828-1211), home to more than 35 dealers of glassware, pottery, primitives, photographs, toys, postcards, and books. Next stop, Asahel Gridley Antiques (217 E. Front St.; 309-829-9615), where collectors can meander through 13 rooms filled with blue-and-white china, paintings, brass candlesticks, jewelry boxes, and a large selection of lighting fixtures.

Worthy of note is the David Davis Mansion (1000 E. Monroe St.; 309-828-1084), a sprawling 1872 Italianate owned by Mr. Davis, a Supreme Court justice from 1866 to 1877 and a close friend of Abraham Lincoln's.

Lodging in the Bloomington area includes a number of charming bed-and-breakfasts like the Burr House (210 E. Chestnut St.; 800-449-4182), a Civil War–era home on the National Register of Historic Places. National chain hotels can also be found here, including the Hampton Inn (604½ IAA Dr.; 800-HAMPTON), which offers weekend getaway packages for summertime visitors to the acclaimed Bloomington Shakespeare Festival. Cafés and restaurants abound in Bloomington; one local favorite is Bistro 2000 (1704 Eastland Dr.; 309-663-0784). Before leaving town, stop by the Apple Barn (RR 4; 309-963-5557), a working orchard open July through December, which boasts delicious ciders, preserves, fresh fruit pies, and even antiques in "Grandma's Cottage" on the second floor.

Midwestern Antiques and Flea Markets, State by State

Illinois

First Presbyterian Rummage Sale

Where > First Presbyterian Church, 700 N. Sheridan Rd.,
Lake Forest

When > First Thursday in May, 7 a.m. to 6 p.m.

Admission > None

For more information > (847) 234-6250

Kane County Flea Market

Where > Kane County Fairgrounds, St. Charles

When > First Sunday and preceding Saturday of
every month; Saturdays 12 to 5 p.m.,
Sundays 7 a.m. to 4 p.m.

Admission > $5

For more information > (630) 377-2252

New Maxwell Street Market

Where > Canal St. between Taylor St. and Depot Pl.,
Chicago

When > Sundays year-round, 7 a.m. to 3 p.m.

Admission > None

For more information > (312) 922-3100

Pecatonica Antique and Flea Market

Where > Winnebago County Fairgrounds, Pecatonica

When > Weekend of the third Sunday in May and
September, 8 a.m. to 5 p.m.

Admission > None

For more information > (800) 238-3587;
www.winnebagocountyfair.com

Sandwich Antiques Market

Where > The Fairgrounds, Sandwich

When > Six Sundays a year, in May through October, 8 a.m. to 4 p.m.

Admission > $5

For more information > (773) 227-4464

Sandy Hollow Antique and Flea Market

Where > 3913 Sandy Hollow Rd., Rockford

When > Weekends year-round, 8 a.m. to 5 p.m.

Admission > None

For more information > (815) 397-6683

INDIANA

Barn and Field Flea Market

Where > Jct. W. 151st and Parrish Aves., Cedarlake

When > Weekends year-round, 8 a.m. to 4 p.m.

Admission > None

For more information > (219) 696-7368

Canaan Fall Festival

Where > Village Square, Canaan

When > Friday, Saturday, and Sunday in September, Fridays and Saturdays 9 a.m. to 10 p.m., Sundays 9 a.m. to 5 p.m.

Admission > None

For more information > (812) 839-4770

Gray Goose Antiques and "Collectable's" Fair

Where > Johnson County Fairgrounds, Franklin

When > Various weekends September through April, 9 a.m. to 4 p.m.

Admission > None

For more information > (317) 881-5719

Indiana Flea Market

Where > Indianapolis State Fairgrounds, Indianapolis

When > Friday, Saturday, and Sunday of every month except August; Fridays 12 to 7 p.m., Saturdays 10 a.m. to 7 p.m., Sundays 11 a.m. to 5 p.m.

Admission > None

For more information > (502) 456-2244;
www.stewartpromotions.com

Tri-State Antique Market

Where > U.S. Rte. 50, Lawrenceburg

When > First Sunday of the month from May through October, 7 a.m. to 3 p.m.; early-bird 6 a.m.

Admission > Early-bird $5, general $2.50

For more information > (513) 738-7256;
www.queencityshows.com

IOWA

Antique Show and Flea Market

Where > Vick's Corner, Jct. Hwy. 9 and 86, Spirit Lake

When > Weekends of Memorial Day, Fourth of July, and Labor Day, 8 a.m. to 6 p.m.

Admission > None

For more information > (712) 336-1912

Collector's Fair

Where > Ottumwa Coliseum, Ottumwa

When > Third weekend in January, March, and November, 9 a.m. to 4 p.m.

Admission > None

For more information > (319) 362-7360

Dubuque Flea Market

Where > Dubuque County Fairgrounds, Dubuque

When > Three Sundays a year, in February, April, and
October, 8 a.m. to 3 p.m.

Admission > $1

For more information > (815) 747-7745;
www.netins.net/showcase/jfkpromo

Midwest Antiques Show

Where > Hawkeye Downs Fairgrounds, Cedar Rapids

When > First Sunday in April and last Sunday in October,
9 a.m to 4 p.m.

Admission > $5

For more information > (319) 643-2065

Sharpless Flea Market

Where > 5049 Herbert Hoover Hwy. NE, exit 249, Iowa City

When > Second Sunday of the month, September through
May, 8 a.m. to 4 p.m.; early-bird 6 a.m.

Admission > Early-bird $4, general $2

For more information > (319) 351-8888

KANSAS

Mid-America Flea Markets

Where > Kansas State Fairgrounds, Hutchinson

When > First Sunday of the month, from October through June,
except February, 9 a.m. to 4 p.m.

Admission > 50¢

For more information > (316) 663-5626;
www.midamericamarkets.com

Mid-America Flea Markets

Where > Kansas Coliseum, Wichita

When > One Sunday every month, except July and August, 9 a.m. to 4 p.m.

Admission > $1

For more information > (316) 663-5626; www.midamericamarkets.com

Old School Flea Market

Where > 511 Commercial St., Welda

When > Wednesday through Monday, 10 a.m. to 6 p.m., except Sundays 12 to 6 p.m.

Admission > None

For more information > (785) 448-3367

Sparks Flea Market

Where > Jct. K-7 Hwy. and Mission Rd., between Troy and Highland

When > Thursday through Sunday, three times a year, in May, July, and September, 7 a.m. to 6 p.m.

Admission > None

For more information > (785) 985-2411

Village Flea Market

Where > 2301 S. Meridian, Wichita

When > Fridays, Saturdays, and Sundays year-round, 9 a.m. to 5 p.m.

Admission > None

For more information > (316) 942-8263

MICHIGAN

Ann Arbor Antiques Market

Where > 5055 Ann Arbor Saline Rd., Ann Arbor

When > One Sunday a month, 7 a.m. to 4 p.m.

Admission > $5

For more information > (850) 984-0122

Armada Flea Market

Where > 25381 Armada Ridge Rd., Richmond

When > Tuesdays and Sundays from mid-April through October, 6 a.m. to 2 p.m.

Admission > None

For more information > (810) 784-9604

Centreville Antiques Market

Where > St. Joseph's County Fairgrounds, Centreville

When > Five times a year, May through October, Sunday 7 a.m. to 3 p.m.

Admission > $4

For more information > (773) 227-4464

Country Fair Flea Market

Where > 20900 Dequindre Blvd., Warren

When > Fridays through Sundays year-round, Fridays 4 to 9 p.m., Saturdays and Sundays 10 a.m. to 6 p.m.

Admission > None

For more information > (810) 757-3740

Flat Rock Historical Society Antique and Flea Market

Where > Flat Rock Speedway, Flat Rock

When > First Sunday in May and October, 8 a.m. to 5 p.m.

Admission > None

For more information > (734) 782-5220

Giant Public Market

Where > 3435 Sheridan Ave., Saginaw

When > Weekends year-round, Saturdays 10 a.m. to 7 p.m., Sundays 10 a.m. to 6 p.m.

Admission > None

For more information > (517) 754-9090

MINNESOTA

85-Mile Garage Sale

Where > Hwy. 61, Lake City

When > First full weekend in May, dawn to dusk

Admission > None

For more information > (651) 345-4123; www.lakecity.org

Downtown Oronoco Gold Rush

Where > Various sites in downtown Oronoco

When > Third weekend in August, dawn to dusk

Admission > None

For more information > (507) 367-4405

Osowski Orchard Road Flea Market

Where > 1479 127 St. NE, Monticello

When > Weekends year-round, 9 a.m. to 5 p.m.

Admission > None

For more information > (612) 295-2121

Shady Hollow Flea Market

Where > Hwy. 59, Detroit Lakes

When > Sundays from Memorial Day through the week after Labor Day, 7 a.m. to 5 p.m.

Admission > None

For more information > (218) 847-9488; www.shadyhollowmarket.com

Summer Set Market

Where > Hwy. 34, Park Rapids

When > Thursdays and Saturdays from Memorial Day through Labor Day, 7 a.m. to 4 p.m.

Admission > None

For more information > (218) 732-5570

Wabasha Flea Market

Where > Jct. Hwy. 61 and Industrial Crt., Wabasha

When > Weekends year-round, 9 a.m. to 5 p.m.

Admission > None

For more information > (651) 565-4767

Wright County Swap Meet

Where > 13594 100th St. NW, Annandale

When > Weekends April through October, 8 a.m. to 2 p.m.

Admission > None

For more information > (320) 274-9005

MISSOURI

Barnhart Flea Market

Where > 6850 Hwy. 61/67, Imperial

When > Weekends year-round, 7 a.m. to 5 p.m.

Admission > None

For more information > (636) 464-5503

Big Pevely Flea Market

Where > 8773 Commercial Blvd., Pevely

When > Weekends year-round, 7 a.m. to 5 p.m.

Admission > None

For more information > (636) 479-5400

VINTAGE
Buttons
•50 EA
(100 minimum)

Colony #1 Flea Market

Where > RR1, Rutledge

When > First and second weekend of the month from March through October, first weekend in November, dawn to dusk

Admission > None

For more information > (660) 434-5504

Joplin Flea Market

Where > Old City Market, Virginia Ave., Joplin

When > Weekends year-round, 8 a.m. to 5 p.m.

Admission > None

For more information > (417) 623-3743

South Elwood Flea Market

Where > 17895 Kentucky Rd., Neosho

When > Weekends year-round, dawn to dusk

Admission > None

For more information > (417) 451-5140

NEBRASKA

Brownville, Nebraska Flea Market

Where > Rte. 136, Brownville

When > Last full weekend in September, 8 a.m. to 5 p.m.

Admission > None

For more information > (402) 825-6001

Walthill Flea Market

Where > Hwy. 75, Walthill

When > First full weekend of the month April to October, dawn to dusk

Admission > None

For more information > (402) 846-9150

North Dakota

Dakota Midwest Flea Market and Antique Show

Where > Mandan Community Center, 901 Division St., Mandan

When > First weekend of every month except January, Saturdays 9 a.m. to 5 p.m., Sundays 10 a.m. to 4 p.m.

Admission > None

For more information > (701) 223-6185

Magic City Flea Market

Where > State Fairgrounds, Minot

When > Second weekend of every month except January and July, 9 a.m. to 4 p.m.

Admission > None

For more information > (701) 852-1289

Ohio

Old Clifton Days Flea Market and Townwide Yard Sale

Where > Various sites in Clifton

When > Weekend after Labor Day, dawn to dusk

Admission > None

For more information > (800) 733-9109

Johnstown Lions Memorial Day Flea Market

Where > Public Square, Johnstown

When > Memorial Day weekend, 6:30 a.m. to 5 p.m.

Admission > None

For more information > (740) 967-4423

Medina Flea Market

Where > Medina County Fairgrounds, 735 Lafayette Rd., Medina

When > Various Sundays year-round, 9 a.m. to 3:30 p.m., early-bird 6 a.m.

Admission > Early-bird $2, general $3

For more information > (330) 723-6083

Paris Flea Market

Where > 6201 N. Dixie Dr., Dayton

When > Sundays mid-April through mid-November, 9 a.m. to 5 p.m.

Admission > None

For more information > (937) 223-0222

Scott's Antique Market

Where > Ohio Exposition Center, Columbus

When > One weekend a month from November through June, Saturdays 9 a.m. to 6 p.m., Sundays 10 a.m. to 4 p.m.

Admission > None

For more information > (740) 569-4112

Urbana Antique Show and Flea Market

Where > Champaign County Fairgrounds, Urbana

When > First full weekend of every month except August, Saturdays 9 a.m. to 4 p.m., Sundays 9:30 a.m. to 3 p.m.

Admission > $1

For more information > (937) 653-6013

OKLAHOMA

Buchanan's Antiques and Collectibles Flea Market

Where > Oklahoma City Fairgrounds, Oklahoma City

When > One weekend a month year-round, 9 a.m. to 5 p.m.,
early-bird Fridays 10 a.m. to 7 p.m.

Admission > Early-bird $10, general $2

For more information > (405) 478-4050

Enid Flea Market

Where > 1821 S. Van Buren, Enid

When > Fridays, Saturdays, and Sundays year-round,
9 a.m. to 6 p.m.

Admission > None

For more information > (580) 864-7612

Mary's Ole Time Swap Meet

Where > Jct. 23rd St. and Midwest Blvd., Oklahoma City

When > Weekends year-round, dawn to dusk

Admission > None

For more information > (405) 427-0051

Tulsa Flea Market

Where > Tulsa Fairgrounds, Jct. 21 St. and Yale, Tulsa

When > Saturdays mid-October through mid-September,
8 a.m. to 5 p.m.

Admission > None

For more information > (918) 744-1386

South Dakota

Sioux Falls Flea Market

Where > Expo Center, Sioux Falls

When > First full weekend of the month except June, July, and August; Saturdays 9 a.m. to 5 p.m., Sundays 11 a.m. to 4 p.m.

Admission > None

For more information > (605) 334-1312

Wisconsin

Adams Flea Market

Where > 556 S. Main St., Adams

When > Weekends year-round, Fourth of July, and holiday Mondays May through October; 6 a.m. to 4 p.m.

Admission > None

For more information > (608) 339-3079

Antique Flea Market

Where > Walworth County Fairgrounds, Elkhorn

When > One Sunday a month from May through September, 7 a.m. to dusk

Admission > None

For more information > (262) 723-5651

Princeton Flea Market

Where > Princeton City Park, Princeton

When > Saturdays April through October, 6 a.m. to 2 p.m.

Admission > None

For more information > (920) 295-3877

Rummage-o-Rama

Where > Wisconsin State Fair Park, 84 St. and Greenfield Ave., Milwaukee

When > One or two weekends a month except June, July, and August, 10 a.m. to 5 p.m.

Admission > $1.75

For more information > (262) 521-2111

Shawano Flea Market

Where > Shawano County Fairgrounds, Shawano

When > Sundays April through October except Labor Day weekend, dawn to 4 p.m.

Admission > None

For more information > (715) 526-9769

For more listings by state, access www.fleamarketguide.com.

Notes

Use these pages to jot down room dimensions, dealers' phone numbers and specialties, or the address of a noteworthy antiques shop you spot.

Notes

Notes

West

Where the Sales Are

Catlin Gabel School Rummage Sale

Where > Portland Exposition Center, Portland

When > First weekend and preceding Thursday and Friday of November, Thursday 5 to 9 p.m., Friday and Saturday 10 a.m. to 6 p.m., Sunday 10 a.m. to 3 p.m.

Admission > None

For more information > (503) 297-1894, ext. 423

Traditional flea markets are not easy to come by in Portland. There are neighborhood-wide garage sales from time to time, and high-end antiques shows three times a year, but no established gathering place for dealers, collectors, and people just unloading their old stuff. Small wonder then that antiques enthusiasts in the area await the annual Catlin Gabel School Rummage Sale with such anticipation. Held each year on the first weekend of November and the Thursday and Friday preceding it, this local school's fund-raiser takes over the Portland Exposition Center and fills it with the donations that have been accepted throughout the year. Although much of the merchandise is of recent vintage—such as secondhand clothes, appliances, and exercise equipment—a good number of antiques and collectibles, including fine china, kitchenware, and books, also make their way into the mix. Part of the fun is not knowing what you might find: Both sailboats and rookie baseball cards have turned up here over the years. The sale runs from Thursday evening (when local antique dealers are in hot pursuit of the sleepers) through Sunday afternoon. If getting there first is not a priority, insiders report that Friday is the best day to shop, before the weekend crowds descend.

You can while away the remainder of the weekend in one of Portland's antiquing havens. The largest and most established area is "Antiques Row" in the Sellwood-Moreland district, which stretches along SE 13th Avenue between Clatsop and Malden Avenues. Local treasure troves include The General Store (7987 SE 13th Ave.; 503-233-1321), Quimby's Arts & Antiques (8535 SE 13th Ave.; 503-235-7460), and Sellwood Peddler Attic Goodies (8065 SE 13th Ave.; 503-235-0946). Neighborhood restaurants range from lively lunchtime eateries like Antique Row Café (8235 SE 13th Ave.; 503-232-2244) to chic nightspots like Caprial's Bistro (7015 SE Milwaukee Ave.; 503-236-6457).

Not far from the shops of Sellwood-Moreland are a number of bed-and-breakfasts, each with a personality all its own. Greek columns and an elegant fountain welcome guests at Portland's White House (1914 NE 22nd Ave.; 800-272-7131), a stately nine-room inn that bears an uncanny resemblance to a certain residence in Washington, D.C. More casual, but entirely comfortable, is the cozy Portland Guest House (1720 NE 15th Ave.; 503-282-1402), where innkeeper Susan Gisvold drops off home-baked treats daily.

Fairgrounds Antiques Market

Where > Arizona State Fairgrounds, Phoenix

When > Third weekend of January, May, September, and November; Saturdays, 9 a.m. to 5 p.m., Sundays 10 a.m. to 4 p.m.

Admission > None

For more information > (800) 678-9987; www.jackblack.com

Since it began in 1986, Phoenix's Fairgrounds Antiques Market has continued to grow. Held four times a year, on the third weekend of January, May, September, and November, this indoor sale regularly attracts anywhere from 200 to 500 vendors as well as thousands of shoppers. Frequent attendees have come to expect a large selection of china dinner services, glassware, cast-iron toys, and other classic antiques. Memorabilia of the Old West are also visible while you're perusing the aisles; items spotted in past years include Western clothing, cowboy figurines, enamelware and pottery bearing illustrations of covered wagons and bucking broncos, and old LPs by cowboy crooners like Frankie Laine and Gene Autry. Textiles—quilts, camp blankets, buggy shawls, and linens—are other categories well represented here.

Collectors should definitely set aside a full day to explore the nearby town of Glendale, about a 15-minute drive from downtown Phoenix. Named one of the top ten antiquing areas in the United States by *USA Today*, Glendale's historic district is home to more than 40 antiques stores, plus a smattering of cafés, tearooms, and gift boutiques. An open-air trolley transports shoppers through the tree-lined streets, connecting neighborhoods like picturesque Catlin Court, distinguished by beautifully restored early-20th-century bungalows, and Old Towne, a quaint area with an old-fashioned Main Street feel to it. Among the delightful shops to be found in Glendale are Antique Treasures (7025 N. 57th Dr.; 623-931-8049), Larry's Antiques (7120 N. 55th Dr.; 623-435-1133), and The Victorian Rose (7015A N. 58th Dr.; 623-435-8251). Old Towne Antiques (7003 N. 58th Ave.; 623-939-8874) specializes in Victorian antiques including furniture, linens, primitives, and what they dub "country kitchen" items. Also on the Old Towne Antiques premises is the Heavenly Tearoom (7003 N. 58th Ave.; 623-847-5100), an ideal rest stop for a traditional

pot of tea with scones and finger sandwiches. From October through May, local craftspeople display textiles, jewelry, découpage, and other handmade creations at the outdoor Market at Murphy Park, in the center of Glendale.

Lodging in the immediate Glendale area includes the Spring Hill Suites (7810 W. Bell Rd.; 623-878-6666) and the 1928 Spanish-style Maricopa Manor (15 W. Pasadena Ave.; 602-274-6302), which offers well-appointed suites and verdant gardens overflowing with bougainvillea.

Santa Monica Airport Outdoor Antique & Collectible Market

SANTA MONICA, CALIFORNIA

Where > South side of Santa Monica Airport, Airport Ave., Santa Monica

When > Fourth Sunday of every month, and the fifth Sunday if there is one, 8 a.m. to 3 p.m.; early-bird 6 to 8 a.m.

Admission > Early-bird $6, general $4

For more information > (323) 933-2511

With the warm California sun beaming down, blue skies overhead, and some 200 dealers offering exceptional antiques and collectibles, you'll find yourself strolling through this show for hours upon hours. Held on the fourth Sunday of every month, and the fifth if there is one, this sale attracts a fair number of celebrities. Some shoppers have even been known to land private planes on the nearby airstrips, peruse the aisles, then take off again with purchases in tow. Vendors at this sale take special care to arrange their booths like small boutiques—you won't find many casually strewn tables full of odds and ends here—so be prepared for a real visual treat. Garden antiques are plentiful, as are painted cottage furnishings and architectural salvage. Even the concession stand has a more refined feeling than at most flea markets; instead of hot dogs and soda pop, you're more likely to find grilled portobello mushrooms and freshly squeezed orange juice.

Santa Monica is a thoroughly walkable city, from the colorful, pedestrian-only Third Street Promenade to stylish Montana Avenue, where a number of antiques and home design shops can be found. Devotees of the "Shabby Chic" look will want to stop by the store that started it all, Rachel Ashwell's Shabby Chic (1013 Montana Ave.; 310-394-1975). Outdoor tables beneath pink-and-white umbrellas lure shoppers to Café Dana (1211 Montana Ave.; 310-394-0815), set back just off the main road in the brick-paved Montana Mews, for afternoon tea. Aficionados of American folk sculpture should schedule a ride on the carousel at the historic Santa Monica Pier: Each of the carousel's 44 steeds and two chariots was carved in 1922 by the famous Philadelphia Toboggan Company.

Lodging in Santa Monica ranges from luxurious beach-front properties like the all-suite Hotel Oceana (849 Ocean Ave.; 800-777-0758), set on a bluff overlooking the Pacific, to smaller, homey properties like the 14-room Channel Road Inn (219 W. Channel Rd.; 310-459-1920). Channel Road's sunny, well-stocked library contains a collection of humorous and touching letters written by the home's original owner— Scottish-born businessman Thomas McCall (1855–1941)—to his youngest daughter.

ALASKA

Anchorage Downtown Saturday Market

Where > Jct. 3rd and E Sts., Anchorage

When > Saturdays mid-May through mid-September,
10 a.m. to 6 p.m.

Admission > None

For more information > (907) 272-5634

ARIZONA

American Park-n-Swap

Where > 3801 E. Washington, Phoenix

When > Weekends year-round, 7 a.m. to 4 p.m.

Admission > None

For more information > (800) 772-0852;
www.americanparknswap.com

Peddler's Pass Flea Market

Where > 6201 E. Hwy. 69, Prescott Valley

When > Weekends year-round, dawn to dusk

Admission > None

For more information > (520) 775-4117

CALIFORNIA

"America's Largest" Antique & Collectible Show

Where > Cow Palace, San Francisco

When > Two weekends a year, in February and September;
Saturdays 8 a.m. to 6 p.m., Sundays 9 a.m. to 5 p.m.

Admission > $5

For more information > (503) 282-0877

Foothill College Flea Market

Where > 12345 El Monte Rd., parking lot 7, Los Altos Hills

When > Third Saturday of every month, 8 a.m. to 3 p.m.

Admission > None

For more information > (650) 948-6417

Golden West College Swap Meet

Where > Golden West College, Huntington Beach

When > Weekends year-round, 8 a.m. to 3 p.m.

Admission > None

For more information > (714) 898-7927

Long Beach Outdoor Antique and Collectible Market

Where > Veteran's Stadium, Long Beach

When > Third Sunday of the month, 8 a.m. to 3 p.m.

Admission > None

For more information > (323) 655-5703

Rose Bowl Flea Market

Where > Rose Bowl, Pasadena

When > Second Sunday of the month, 9 a.m. to 3 p.m.,
early-bird 7 a.m.

Admission > Early-bird $10, general $6

For more information > (323) 560-7469

COLORADO

Colorado Springs Flea Market

Where > 5225 E. Platte Ave., Colorado Springs

When > Weekends year-round, 7 a.m. to 4 p.m.

Admission > $1

For more information > (719) 380-8599

Lafayette Flea Market

Where > 130 E. Spaulding, Lafayette

When > Every day, 10 a.m. to 6 p.m.

Admission > None

For more information > (303) 665-0433

Mile High Flea Market

Where > Jct. I-76 and E. 88th Ave., Denver

When > Wednesdays, Saturdays, and Sundays year-round, 7 a.m. to 5 p.m.

Admission > None

For more information > (800) 861-9900

HAWAII

Hawaii All-Collectors Show and Sale

Where > Blaisdell Exhibition Hall, Honolulu

When > Third weekend and preceding Friday in July; Friday 4 to 9 p.m., Saturday 11 a.m. to 9 p.m., Sunday, 11 a.m. to 5 p.m.

Admission > $3.75

For more information > (808) 941-9754; www.ukulele.com

IDAHO

Cascade Flea Market

Where > Cascade Airport, Cascade

When > Weekends mid-May through early October, 9 a.m. to 6 p.m.

Admission > None

For more information > (208) 382-3600

Spectra's Flea Market

Where > Western Idaho Fairgrounds, 5610 Glenwood, Boise

When > Weekends mid-September through March,
9 a.m. to 6 p.m.

Admission > $1

For more information > (208) 939-6426

MONTANA

Prairie Flea Market

Where > Prairie Drive-In Theater, Terry

When > Saturdays in late June and mid-August, 8 a.m. to 3 p.m.

Admission > None

For more information > (406) 635-4444

NEVADA

Broadacres Open Air Swap Meet

Where > 2960 Las Vegas Blvd., North Las Vegas

When > Fridays, Saturdays, and Sundays year-round,
6:30 a.m. to dusk

Admission > None

For more information > (702) 642-3777

El Rancho Flea Market

Where > 555 El Rancho Dr., Sparks

When > Weekends year-round, summer 6 a.m. to 4:30 p.m.,
winter 7 a.m. to dusk

Admission > None

For more information > (775) 331-3227

New Mexico

Farmington Flea Market

Where > 7701 E. Main St., Farmington

When > Fridays, Saturdays, and Sundays year-round, summer 6 a.m. to 8 p.m., winter 7 a.m. to 7 p.m.

Admission > None

For more information > (505) 325-3129

New Mexico State Fair Flea Market

Where > New Mexico State Fairgrounds, Albuquerque

When > Weekends year-round, except during State Fair, 7 a.m. to 5 p.m.

Admission > None

For more information > (505) 265-1791

Oregon

"America's Largest" Antique & Collectible Sale

Where > Portland Exposition Center, Portland

When > Three weekends a year, in March, July, and October; Saturdays 8 a.m. to 6 p.m., Sundays 9 a.m. to 5 p.m.

Admission > None

For more information > (503) 282-0877

Medford Giant Flea Market

Where > 1701 S. Pacific Hwy., Medford

When > One Sunday a month year-round, 9 a.m. to 4 p.m.

Admission > None

For more information > (541) 772-8211

Sumpter Flea Market

Where > 400 SE Ibex St., Sumpter

When > Weekends of Memorial Day, Fourth of July, and
Labor Day, 8 a.m. to 5 p.m.

Admission > None

For more information > (541) 894-2314

UTAH

Antique Collectors Fair

Where > South Towne Exposition Center, 9575 S. State St., Sandy

When > Three weekends a year, in February, April, and November;
Saturdays 10 a.m. to 6 p.m., Sundays 10 a.m. to 5 p.m.

Admission > None

For more information > (801) 364-1898; www.utmart.com

Redwood Swap Meet

Where > 3688 S. Redwood Rd., Salt Lake City

When > Weekends year-round, 8 a.m. to 4 p.m.

Admission > 50¢

For more information > (801) 973-6060

WASHINGTON

"America's Largest" Antique & Collectible Sale

Where > Tacoma Dome, Tacoma

When > Three weekends a year, in January, June, and October;
Saturdays 8 a.m. to 6 p.m., Sundays 9 a.m. to 5 p.m.

Admission > None

For more information > (503) 282-0877

GUIDE TO THE BEST FLEA MARKETS

Bridge Street Marketplace Antiques

Where > 1342 Bridge St., Clarkston

When > Tuesdays, Thursdays, and Fridays year-round, 12:30 to 5:30 p.m., Saturdays 10 a.m. to 4 p.m.

Admission > None

For more information > (509) 751-9939; www.highway12antiques.com

Fremont Sunday Market

Where > Jct. N. 34th St. and Fremont Ave., Seattle

When > Sundays May through October, 10 a.m. to 5 p.m.

Admission > None

For more information > (206) 781-6776

Lakeside School Rummage Sale

Where > Stadium Exhibition Center, between Seahawks Stadium and Safeco Field, Seattle

When > Usually the first weekend and preceding Friday in March, Friday and Saturday 10 a.m. to 6 p.m., Sunday 10 a.m. to 2 p.m.

Admission > None

For more information > (206) 440-2740; www.lakesideschool.org

Puget Park Swap-o-Rama

Where > 13020 Meridian Ave. S., Everett

When > Weekends April through October, 9 a.m. to 3:30 p.m.

Admission > None

For more information > (425) 337-1435

WYOMING

Antique Show and Sale

Where > Central Wyoming Fairgrounds, Casper

When > First full weekend in June and October, Saturdays
10 a.m. to 5 p.m., Sundays 10 a.m. to 4 p.m.

Admission > None

For more information > (307) 234-6663

Avenues Antiques & Collectibles

Where > 315 ½ E. 7th Ave., Cheyenne

When > Every day, 12 to 5 p.m.

Admission > None

For more information > (307) 635-5600

Laramie Antiques Show

Where > Albany County Fairgrounds, Laramie

When > Third weekend in August, Saturdays 10 a.m. to 6 p.m.,
Sundays 10 a.m. to 4 p.m.

Admission > $3

For more information > (800) 571-6615;
www.traylorantiqueshows.com

Mangy Moose Antique Show and Sale

Where > Teton Village, Jackson Hole

When > Two weekends a year, in July and August,
9 a.m. to 6 p.m.

Admission > None

For more information > (208) 345-0755

For more listings by state, access www.fleamarketguide.com.

Notes

Use these pages to jot down room dimensions, dealers' phone numbers and specialties, or the address of a noteworthy antiques shop you spot.

_____

_____

_____

_____

_____

_____

_____

_____

_____

_____

_____

_____

_____

_____

_____

_____

_____

_____

_____

Notes

_____

_____

_____

_____

_____

_____

_____

_____

_____

_____

_____

_____

_____

_____

_____

_____

_____

_____

_____

Notes

Canada

Where the Sales Are

70-Mile Coastal Yard Sale

CHARLOTTETOWN, PRINCE EDWARD ISLAND

Where > Sites along and around Rte. 1, Charlottetown

When > One weekend a year in mid- to late September, dawn to dusk

Admission > None

For more information > (888) 734-7529

You may have attended a townwide yard sale before, but that experience will likely pale in comparison once you've tried the event Prince Edward Island style. Held over the course of a weekend in mid- to late September, the 70-Mile Coastal Yard Sale is a relatively new one on the antiquing circuit, having started in 1999. The first stop for all shoppers is Prince Edward Island's Visitor Information Center (178 Water St.; 902-368-4444) in Charlottetown, the island's main commercial hub. Here you can pick up a brochure (your treasure map for the day) showing the sale's 150 to 200 participating sites. Finds here come in all shapes and sizes: An early-19th-century calico girl's dress might just lay hidden among the OshKosh B'Gosh, a highly collectible 1940s juice glass amid simple tumblers, or a rare brooch under a heap of faux pearls.

In addition to its picture-perfect scenery, Prince Edward Island is also known as the birthplace of Anne Shirley, heroine of the beloved 1908 children's classic *Anne of Green Gables*. Many of the sites described in the book—like the little town of Cavendish where the farmhouse that inspired Green Gables

still stands (Rte. 6; 902-963-3370)—have become tourist hotspots. To avoid the crowds, Anne fans can also explore Prince Edward Island's less-traveled rural backroads, which bring author Lucy Maud Montgomery's poetic descriptions of the island to life. Collectors will relish the treasure troves to be found in both barns and storefronts around the island, like A-1 Collectibles (Rte. 1, N. Bedeque; 902-887-3555) and Details Past and Present (166 Richmond St., Charlottetown; 902-892-2233).

Many people consider late September to be one of the best times to visit Prince Edward Island. The weather is still warm, most of the peak-season travelers have gone home, and a good number of the shops, hotels, and restaurants that close for the winter remain open through the end of the month. Accommodations range from old-style resorts like the 15-room,

20-cottage Shaw's Hotel (Rte. 15, Brackley Beach; 902-672-2022) to cozy bed-and-breakfasts like the Victoria Village Inn (22 Howard St., Victoria-by-the-Sea; 902-658-2483). Don't leave without sampling one of the island's famous family-style lobster lunches and suppers, such as the ones hosted by St. Ann's Church (Rte. 224, St. Ann's, Hope River; 902-621-0635).

Sunday Antiques Market

KINGSTON, ONTARIO

Where > Market Square behind City Hall, Kingston

When > Sundays May through October, dawn to dusk

Admission > None

For more information > (613) 544-2495

Set on the shores of Lake Ontario at the mouth of the St. Lawrence River, Kingston may be one of Canada's best-kept secrets. Not only a city of great natural and architectural beauty, Kingston is also a collector's paradise. Tiny antiques shops, brimming with keepsakes are sprinkled liberally about the town, and the local flea market has thrived here for more than 20 years. A relatively small sale, with an average of 25 to 30 dealers, Kingston's Sunday Antiques Market rewards visitors with consistently wonderful merchandise. Dusty paintings that may just be undiscovered works of an important 19th-century artist, antique instruments, porcelain teacups in a multitude of patterns, furniture, textiles, and Victorian autograph albums are but a few of the things you might uncover at the market.

Before hitting the antiques shops, architecture enthusiasts will want to take a walking tour of downtown. Pick up a brochure for a self-guided walking tour from the Tourist Information Office (209 Ontario St.; 613-548-4415). Known as "the Limestone City" for its rich local quarries, Kingston boasts an abundance of elegant limestone homes and commercial buildings, many dating back hundreds of years. Now it's time

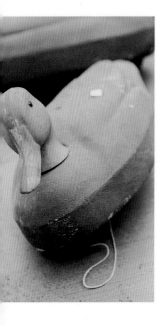

to shop. Looking for formal 18th- and 19th-century furniture? Head to Cellar Door Antiques (359 Barrie St.; 613-546-7447). Pressed glass and oil lamps? Pangborn's Antiques (3 Calderwood Dr.; 613-548-4989) offers a good array of choices. In addition to an ample mix of 19th- and early-20th-century goods, Abbey Dawn Quilts & Antiques (1619 Abbey Dawn Rd.; 613-542-6247) also harbors a large selection of old gramophones.

A few of the old homes in town have even been turned into bed-and-breakfasts, including the three-guest-room c. 1799 A Stone's Throw B&B (21 Earl St.; 613-544-6089).

The line may be long, but many locals wouldn't miss Sunday brunch at Chez Piggy (68R Princess St.; 613-549-7673). If you'd like to combine lunch with more sightseeing, pack a picnic and head for the free ferry ride to Wolfe Island (ferry dock at the Jct. of Queen and Ontario Sts.); the 25-minute trip offers unparalleled views of the breathtaking Thousand Islands.

At the end of the day, lay your head on a pillow at the elegant Belvedere Hotel (141 King St. E.; 800-559-0584). While a host of amenities recommend the Belvedere, one in particular will attract collectors: an in-house antiques shop—Antiques & Uniques (613-548-1565)—filled with porcelain, crystal, and silver, as well as Victorian and Art Deco furniture.

Calgary Summer Antiques Show

Where > Canada Olympic Park, Calgary

When > One weekend a year, in late June or early July, Saturday
9 a.m. to 5 p.m., Sunday 10 a.m. to 5 p.m.

Admission > None

For more information > (800) 667-0619

Though many years have passed since the 1988 Winter Olympics, the competitive spirit is still alive and well in Calgary. You'll see it in the collectors who flock here for the annual Summer Antiques Show, held in June or July at the Olympic Park. Lines form long before the show's 9 a.m. Saturday opening, and foot traffic remains steady throughout the course of the weekend. Billed as western Canada's only outdoor antiques extravaganza, the Summer Antiques Show draws about 150 dealers from around the country. Shoppers who scan the varied offerings laid out beneath large tents will notice a good mix of both the items that are typical of the Western provinces, (rugged country cupboards, cowboy and ranching memorabilia, and native Canadian crafts and artifacts) as well as English antiques (china, silver, linens, and mahogany furniture).

After sifting through the last booth at the show, collectors often heed the siren call of Calgary's Inglewood neighborhood,

where a number of antiques stores are clustered along 9th Avenue SE near 12th Street. Here you'll find the Inglewood Florist (1218B 9th Ave. SE; 403-264-9463), a pretty shop in which kitchen tins, toleware, toys, and other collectibles share shelf space with fresh and dried flower displays. Fireplace mantels, blanket chests, jelly cupboards, pine flooring, enamelware, and old iron hay forks are just a few of the treasures waiting to be discovered at Junktiques, Ltd. (1226 9th Ave. SE; 403-263-0619). Haven't found what you're looking for yet? Try the 10,000-square-foot Junktiques warehouse, called Woodwise (4711 13th St. NE, #102; 403-291-4493).

One of Calgary's most charming bed-and-breakfasts is located in the heart of Inglewood—the Inglewood Bed and Breakfast (1006 8th Ave. SE; 403-262-6570). Innkeepers Valinda Larson and Helmut Schoderbock have furnished each of the three guest rooms in this Queen Anne–style house with country furniture and antiques. Closer to the center of Calgary, the large 1914 Palliser Hotel (133 9th Ave. SW;  800-441-1414) represents a touch of old-world glamour. For brunch, lunch, or dinner, try one of Inglewood's international eateries or hop a cab for a quick ride to 17th Avenue, anywhere between 5th and 10th Streets, the city's bustling café and bistro district. The Painted Pony Antique Center (614 17th Ave. SW; 403-229-1671), which has 20 dealers under one roof, is also located nearby.

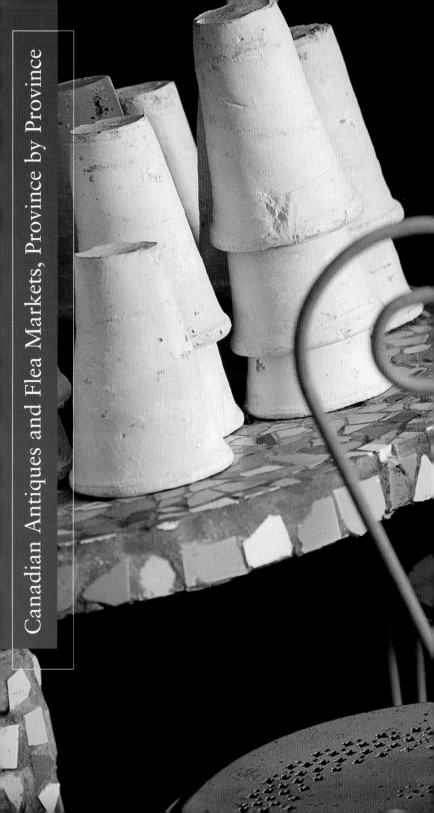

ALBERTA

Crossroads Market

Where > 1235 26th Ave. SE, Calgary

When > Weekends year-round, 9 a.m. to 5 p.m.

Admission > None

For more information > (403) 291-5208

Hillhurst-Sunnyside Community Center Flea Market

Where > 1320 5th Ave. NW, Calgary

When > Sundays year-round, 7 a.m. to 3 p.m.

Admission > None

For more information > (403) 283-1400

BRITISH COLUMBIA

Best of the West Antique Expo

Where > Tradex Exhibition Centre, Abbotsford

When > Two weekends a year, in July and November, Saturdays 9 a.m. to 5 p.m., Sundays 10 a.m. to 5 p.m.

Admission > None

For more information > (800) 667-0619

Vancouver Flea Market

Where > 703 Terminal Ave., Vancouver

When > Weekends year-round, 9 a.m. to 5 p.m.

Admission > None

For more information > (604) 685-0666

New Brunswick

NBAAC Flea Market

Where > Princess Louise Park, Sussex

When > One Friday through Sunday in August, 8 a.m. to 8 p.m.

Admission > $2 Cdn

For more information > (506) 684-4394

Nova Scotia

Windsor Country Fair Flea Market

Where > Hwy. 101, Windsor

When > Weekends mid-June through early September,
9:30 a.m. to 4:30 p.m.

Admission > None

For more information > (902) 798-0000

Ontario

Aberfoyle Antique Market

Where > RR 3, Guelph

When > Sundays late April through late October,
8 a.m. to 4 p.m.

Admission > None

For more information > (519) 763-1077

Bentley's Antiques & Collectibles Flea Market

Where > 7 Cleopatra Dr., Ottawa

When > Sundays year-round, 9 a.m. to 5 p.m.

Admission > None

For more information > (613) 225-5613

Christie Classic Antique Show

Where > Christie Conservation Area, Dundas

When > Two Saturdays a year, May and September,
8 a.m. to 5 p.m.

Admission > None

For more information > (888) 594-9297

Stouffville Country Market

Where > 12555 Tenth Line N., Stouffville

When > Weekends year-round, Saturdays 8 a.m. to 4 p.m.,
Sundays 9 a.m. to 4 p.m.

Admission > None

For more information > (905) 640-3813

Toronto Sunday Market

Where > 92 Front St. E., Toronto

When > Sundays year-round, dawn to dusk

Admission > None

For more information > (416) 410-1310

QUEBEC

Marché aux Puces de Cing Étoiles

Where > Exit 78 off Autoroute 10, Bromont

When > Sundays early May through late October, 7 a.m. to 5 p.m.

Admission > None

For more information > (514) 875-5500

For more listings by province, access www.fleamarketguide.com or
www.antiqueshowscanada.com.

Notes

Use these pages to jot down room dimensions, dealers' phone numbers and specialties, or the address of a noteworthy antiques shop you spot.

_____

_____

_____

_____

_____

_____

_____

_____

_____

_____

_____

_____

_____

_____

_____

_____

Notes

Notes

Notes

The Top 100 Antiques and Flea Markets in North America

Here's the list of our favorite flea markets from coast to coast, listed alphabetically by state and then province.

ALABAMA

> Birmingham Fairgrounds Flea Market, Birmingham

> World's Longest Yard Sale—450 Miles, starts in Gadsden and proceeds north through Tennessee and Kentucky

ARIZONA

> Fairgrounds Antiques Market, Phoenix

ARKANSAS

> Thackerland Flea Market, Judsonia

CALIFORNIA

> Long Beach Outdoor Antique and Collectible Market, Long Beach

> Rose Bowl Flea Market, Pasadena

> Santa Monica Airport Outdoor Antique & Collectible Market, Santa Monica

COLORADO

> Lafayette Flea Market, Lafayette

CONNECTICUT

> Farmington Antiques Weekend, Farmington

> Elephant's Trunk Bazaar, New Milford

> Woodbury Antiques and Flea Market, Woodbury

DELAWARE

> New Castle Farmers Market, New Castle

WASHINGTON, D.C.

> Capitol Hill Flea Market

> Georgetown Flea Market

FLORIDA

> Florida Twin Markets, Mt. Dora

> Webster Westside Flea Market, Webster

> Piccadilly Antique and Collectible Fair, West Palm Beach

GEORGIA

> Lakewood Antiques Market, Atlanta

> Scotts Antique Market Show, Atlanta

IDAHO

> Cascade Flea Market, Cascade

ILLINOIS

> Third Sunday Market, Bloomington

> First Presbyterian Rummage Sale, Lake Forest

> Sandwich Antiques Market, Sandwich

> Kane County Flea Market, St. Charles

INDIANA

> Barn and Field Flea Market, Cedarlake

> Gray Goose Antiques and "Collectable's" Fair, Franklin

> Tri-State Antique Market, Lawrenceburg

IOWA

> Midwest Antiques Show, Cedar Rapids

> Sharpless Flea Market, Iowa City

> Collector's Paradise Flea Market, What Cheer

KANSAS

> Mid-America Flea Markets, Hutchinson

> Sparks Flea Market, Troy

KENTUCKY

> Kentucky Flea Market, Louisville

LOUISIANA

> Jefferson Flea Market, Kenner

> Community Flea Market, New Orleans

MAINE

> Wiscasset Old Jail Outdoor Antiques Show and Sale, Wiscasset

> Montsweag Flea Market, Woolwich

MARYLAND

> Bonnie Brae Flea Market, Edgewood

MASSACHUSETTS

> Charlton Antiques, Charlton Antique and Flea Market

> Brimfield Antique Shows, Brimfield

MICHIGAN

> Ann Arbor Antiques Market, Ann Arbor

> Centreville Antiques Market, Centreville

> Flat Rock Historical Society Antique and Flea Market, Flat Rock

MINNESOTA

> Downtown Oronoco Gold Rush, Oronoco

MISSISSIPPI

> Fairgrounds Antique Flea Market, Jackson

MISSOURI

> Big Pevely Flea Market, Pevely

NEBRASKA

> Brownville, Nebraska Flea Market, Brownville

NEW HAMPSHIRE

> Grandview Flea Market, Derry

> Antiques Week in New Hampshire, Manchester

NEW JERSEY

> Atlantique City, Atlantic City

> Columbus Farmer's Market, Columbus

> Lambertville Antiques Market, Lambertville

> Ocean Grove Flea Market, Ocean Grove

NEW MEXICO

> New Mexico State Fair Flea Market, Albuquerque

NEW YORK

> Madison-Bouckville Outdoor Antiques Show, Bouckville

> The Annex Antiques Fair and Flea Market, New York City

> Triple Pier Expo, New York City

> Stormville Airport Antique Show and Flea Market, Stormville

NORTH CAROLINA

> Metrolina Expo Antiques & Antique Collectibles Market, Charlotte

> Fairgrounds Flea Market, Raleigh

NORTH DAKOTA

> Dakota Midwest Flea Market and Antique Show, Mandan

OHIO

> Scott's Antique Market, Columbus

> Springfield Antique Show and Flea Market, Springfield

OKLAHOMA

> Mary's Ole Time Swap Meet, Oklahoma City

> Tulsa Flea Market, Tulsa

OREGON

> Catlin Gabel School Rummage Sale, Portland

PENNSYLVANIA

> Renninger's Antiques Market, Adamstown

> Renninger's Antique Market #2, Kutztown

> Collector's Cove, Sciota

RHODE ISLAND

> General Stanton Flea Market, Charleston

SOUTH CAROLINA

> Lowcountry Market, Charleston

SOUTH DAKOTA

> Sioux Falls Flea Market, Sioux Falls

TENNESSEE

> Flea Market at the Nashville Fairgrounds, Nashville

TEXAS

> Austin Country Flea Market, Austin

> First Monday Trade Days, Canton

> Antiques Week in Round Top, Round Top

VERMONT

> Charlotte Flea Market, Charlotte

> Manchester Flea Market, Manchester Center

> Wilmington Outdoor Antique and Flea Market, Wilmington

VIRGINIA

> Manor Mart Flea Market, Fredericksburg

> Richmond Big Flea, Richmond

WASHINGTON

> Fremont Sunday Market, Seattle

> Lakeside School Rummage Sale, Seattle

WEST VIRGINIA

> Harpers Ferry Flea Market, Harpers Ferry

WISCONSIN

> Adams Flea Market, Adams

> Princeton Flea Market, Princeton

WYOMING

> Antique Show and Sale, Casper

CANADA

ALBERTA

> Calgary Summer Antiques Show, Calgary

> Hillhurst-Sunnyside Community Center Flea Market, Calgary

BRITISH COLUMBIA

> Best of the West Antique Expo, Abbotsford

> Vancouver Flea Market, Vancouver

NEW BRUNSWICK

> NBAAC Flea Market, Sussex

NOVA SCOTIA

> Windsor Country Fair Flea Market, Windsor

ONTARIO

> Christie Classic Antique Show, Dundas

> Aberfoyle Antique Market, Guelph

> Sunday Antiques Market, Kingston

> Stouffville Country Market, Stouffville

> Toronto Sunday Market, Toronto

PRINCE EDWARD ISLAND

> 70-Mile Coastal Yard Sale, Charlottetown

QUEBEC

> Marché aux Puces de Cing Étoiles, Bromont

Notes

GUIDE TO THE BEST FLEA MARKETS

Notes

_____

_____

_____

_____

_____

_____

_____

_____

_____

_____

_____

_____

_____

_____

_____

_____

_____

Photography Credits

90	Jim Bastardo
100-101	Jim Bastardo
102	Marie Proeller
106	Marie Proeller
107	Jim Bastardo
109	Steve Randazzo
110	Keith Scott Morton
115	Alan Richardson
120	Marie Proeller
130-131	Keith Scott Morton
132	Marie Proeller
136	Jim Bastardo
137	Keith Scott Morton
138	Alan Richardson
140	Keith Scott Morton
141	Alan Richardson
141	Alan Richardson
142	Keith Scott Morton
147	Keith Scott Morton
150	Keith Scott Morton
156-157	Marie Proeller
159	Marie Proeller
160	Keith Scott Morton
162	Keith Scott Morton
163	Alan Richardson
165	Keith Scott Morton
166	Keith Scott Morton
167	Jim Bastardo
168	Keith Scott Morton
176-177	Marie Proeller
180	Keith Scott Morton
185	Jim Bastardo
186	Jim Bastardo
192	Marie Proeller
Back Cover	(all) Keith Scott Morton